OUR ENEMY, THE STATE

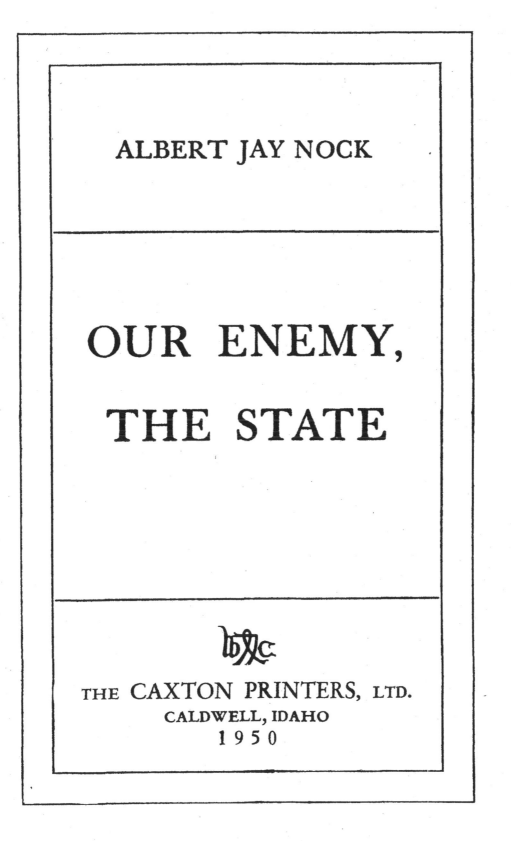

ALBERT JAY NOCK

OUR ENEMY,
THE STATE

THE CAXTON PRINTERS, LTD.
CALDWELL, IDAHO
1950

First printing, 1935
Second printing, 1946
Third printing, 1950

Large Print Edition published 2012 by Skyler J. Collins.
Visit: www.skylerjcollins.com

ISBN-13: 978-1478385004
ISBN-10: 1478385006

IN MEMORIAM
EDMUND CADWALADER EVANS
A SOUND ECONOMIST, ONE OF
THE FEW WHO UNDERSTAND
THE NATURE OF THE STATE

INTRODUCTION

HALF A century ago, as I was struggling to articulate a social and political philosophy with which my inner voices could find approval, I discovered one of my earliest introductions to what has since come to be known as libertarian thought. I had read—and enjoyed—classical philosophers John Locke, John Stuart Mill, the Stoics, and others who took seriously the plight of the individual at the hands of political systems. Discovering the writings of H.L. Mencken, during the early days of my inquiries, introduced me to a number of contemporary critics of governmental behavior. It was at this time that I read a book, titled *Our Enemy the State*, written by Albert Jay Nock, that began the real transformation of my thinking. I soon became less interested in the pursuit of abstract philosophic reasoning, and increasingly focused on the realpolitik of political systems.

A major problem with political philosophies is that they involve the playing out of the abstract thoughts of their authors. Are the differing visions of a "state of nature" as seen by Hobbes, Rousseau, or Locke, grounded in empirical studies of the history of stateless societies or only the projections of the life experiences, intuitive speculations, indoctrinations, the collective unconscious, and other internally generated influences upon the mind of the writer? As our understanding of the world is grounded in subjectivity, the same question needs to be asked of anyone engaged in speculative philosophy: is it possible to stand outside our own minds and comment upon the world free of the content of our own thinking? Was Heisenberg right in telling us that the observer is an indispensable ingredient in what is being observed? We are easily seduced into confusing the reality of political systems with our expectations as to how such systems ought to work.

Who was this observer I had just discovered? Albert Jay Nock began his career as an Episcopal priest, later turning to journalism.

At different times, he wrote for the magazines *The Nation* and *Freeman*, publications with different perspectives than their current versions. A self-described Jeffersonian and Georgist, he was an articulate spokesman for classical liberalism; an advocate of free markets, private property, who had a strong distrust of power. He wrote at a time when the concept of "liberalism" was being intellectually and politically corrupted into its antithesis of the state-directed society; and he was troubled by the detrimental effect such a transformation would have on both individuals and the culture when the resulting debasement of character and behavior became accepted as the norm.

Nock had an abiding interest in the epistemological question that asks how we know what it is we know, and how changes in our thinking generate the outward modifications that occur in our world. In his classic *Memoirs of a Superfluous Man*, he observed that "the most significant thing about [a man] is what he thinks; and significant also is how he came to think it, why he continued to think it, or, if he did not continue, what the influences were which caused him to change his mind."

Albert Jay Nock was what, in my youth, would have been described as an exponent of a "liberal arts" education. He understood not only that "ideas have consequences"—a proposition later expounded upon by Richard Weaver—but that organizations have a certain dynamic which, when mobilized, can generate unexpected consequences. He acknowledged the pursuit of individual self-interest as a principal motivating factor, but saw how corporate and political interests can combine to promote such interests, coercively, at the expense of others.

Nock's intellectual development was greatly influenced by the works of the German economist and sociologist, Franz Oppenheimer. Nock focused much of his attention on Oppenheimer's analysis of the two principal means—expounded upon in *Der Staat*—by which human needs can be met. Satisfying such needs through the exercise of "one's own labor and the equivalent exchange of one's own labor for the labor of others," Oppenheimer defined as the "economic means." By contrast, pursuing such interests through "the unrequited appropriation of the labor of others" he termed the "political means." Nock elaborates upon Oppenheimer's thesis to describe how the state actually works. Because people tend to act with "the least possible exertion" in pursuing their ends, they will tend to prefer the political to the economic means, a trait that has produced the modern corporate-state—or what Nock referred to as the "merchant-State."

The efforts of earlier political philosophers to explain the origins of the state either as an expression of "divine will," or the product of an alleged "social contract," begin to melt away when confronted by Nock's realism. He tells us that the state has its genesis not in some highly principled pursuit of a "common will" to resist some imagined perverse human nature, but in nothing more elevated than "conquest and confiscation." He echoes Voltaire's observation that "the art of government consists in taking as much money as possible from one class of the citizens to give to the other." The Watergate-era mantra "follow the money" reverberates this more prosaic theme.

Those who chide critics of the state as being "idealistic" or "utopian" must, themselves, answer for their visionary faith that state power could be made to restrain itself. As Nock understood, and as more recent history confirms, it is those who believe that written constitutions can protect the individual from the exercise of state power who hold to a baseless idealism, particularly when it is the state's judicial powers of interpretation that define the range of such authority. Words are abstractions that never correlate with what they purport to describe and must, therefore, be interpreted. Supreme Court decisions continue to affirm Nock's realistic assessment that "anything may be made to mean anything." The twentieth century, alone, provided thinkers such as Nock with a perspective that allowed them to see how the earlier speculations about the nature of the state actually played out. The post-9/11 years have seen a wholesale retreat by the

American government from the illusion of limited government, with constitutional prescriptions for and proscriptions against state power widely ignored. Anthony deJasay has added his critique of the imaginary nature of limited government, by observing that "collective choice is never independent of what significant numbers of individuals wish it to be." Has history shown that political systems and the citizenry retain the sense of mutuality that is implicit in the "contract" theory that supposedly underlies the modern state? Does the avowed purpose of political systems to protect the lives, liberty, and property interests of individuals remain intact?

The modern state increasingly manifests itself as the ill it was the purpose of centuries-old philosophies to identify, and of constitutional systems to prevent. This raises the question whether the very existence of the state, with its self-interested exercise of a monopoly on the use of force, could portend other than the continuing cycles of wars, repression, economic dislocations, and other forms of collective conflict and disorder? Will today's young minds, desirous of understanding the reality rather than just a theory of politics grounded in hope, be able to resist a shift in thinking such as is offered by Nock and others who offer explanations for statism grounded in principled pragmatism?

Such a question brings us to a consideration of Nock's purposes in writing. He had no interest in political reforms, seeing such efforts as superficial in nature. Neither was he motivated by a desire to educate mass-minded men and women, as such people lacked both the depth of character and the intellectual capacity to understand the principles underlying "the humane life." He saw his task, rather, as being to care for those he called "the Remnant," those independent men and women whose intellectual and emotional inquisitiveness provide them a profound understanding of such principles. Unlike mass-minded persons who are easily manipulated and mobilized in service to various institutional causes, the Remnant remain skeptical of proselytizers who seek converts to ideologies, or who desire to save mankind.

Trying to find members of the Remnant will be futile, Nock tells us, for it is they who will seek out like-minded spirits. Nock sees his role as providing the support and nurturing to such individuals who will, once the civilization has collapsed, be the ones to "build up a new society" on the basis of their understanding of the "august order of nature." For such people alone, Nock tells us, was this book written.

Our Enemy the State was first published in 1935, when the economic consequences of the New Deal were beginning to be felt. In his preface to the 1946 printing of this work, Nock's friend, Frank Chodorov, tells us that, in 1943, Nock spoke of writing a second edition to elaborate on these economic effects. In the summer of 1945, however, Nock died without accomplishing this task. Even without such modifications, Chodorov observes that "Our Enemy the State needs no support," and stands as a powerful indictment of political systems.

BUTLER SHAFFER
July 2009

Be it or be it not true that Man is shapen in iniquity and conceived in sin, it is unquestionably true that Government is begotten of aggression, and by aggression.

HERBERT SPENCER, 1850.

This is the gravest danger that today threatens civilization: State intervention, the absorption of all spontaneous social effort by the State; that is to say, of spontaneous historical action, which in the long-run sustains, nourishes and impels human destinies.

JOSÉ ORTEGA Y GASSET, 1922.

It [the State] has taken on a vast mass of new duties and responsibilities; it has spread out its powers until they penetrate to every act of the citizen, however secret; it has begun to throw around its operations the high dignity and impeccability of a State religion; its agents become a separate and superior caste, with authority to bind and loose, and their thumbs in every pot. But it still remains, as it was in the beginning, the common enemy of all well-disposed, industrious and decent men.

HENRY L. MENCKEN, 1926.

PREFACE TO SECOND EDITION

When OUR ENEMY THE STATE appeared in 1935, its literary merit rather than its philosophic content attracted attention to it. The times were not ripe for an acceptance of its predictions, still less for the argument on which these predictions were based. Faith in traditional frontier individualism had not yet been shaken by the course of events. Against this faith the argument that the same economic forces which in all times and in all nations drive toward the ascendancy of political power at the expense of social power were in operation here made little headway. That is, the feeling that "it cannot happen here" was too difficult a hurdle for the book to overcome.

By the time the first edition had run out, the development of public affairs gave the argument of the book ample testimony. In less than a decade it was evident to many Americans that their country is not immune from the philosophy which had captured European thinking. The times were proving Mr. Nock's thesis, and by irresistable word-of-mouth advertising a demand for the book began to manifest itself just when it was no longer available. And the plates had been put to war purposes.

In 1943 he had a second edition in mind. I talked with him several times about it, urging him to elaborate on the economic ideas, since these, it seemed to me, were inadequately developed for the reader with a limited knowledge of political economy. He agreed that this ought to be done, but in a separate book, or in a second part of his book, and suggested that I try my hand at it. Nothing came of the matter because of the war. He died on August 19, 1945.

This volume is an exact duplication of the first edition. He intended to make some slight changes, principally, as he told me, in the substitution of current illustrations for those which might carry less weight with the younger reader. As for the sequel stressing economics, this will have to be done. At any rate, OUR ENEMY THE STATE needs no support.

FRANK CHODOROV

New York City, May 28th, 1946

OUR ENEMY, THE STATE

1

IF WE look beneath the surface of our public affairs, we can discern one fundamental fact, namely: a great redistribution of power between society and the State. This is the fact that interests the student of civilization. He has only a secondary or derived interest in matters like price-fixing, wage-fixing, inflation, political banking, "agricultural adjustment," and similar items of State policy that fill the pages of newspapers and the mouths of publicists and politicians. All these can be run up under one head. They have an immediate and temporary importance, and for this reason they monopolize public attention, but they all come to the same thing; which is, an increase of State power and a corresponding decrease of social power.

It is unfortunately none too well understood that, just as the State has no money of its own, so it has no power of its own. All the power it has is what society gives it, plus what it confiscates from time to time on one pretext or another; there is no other source from which State power can be drawn. Therefore every assumption of State power, whether by gift or seizure, leaves society with so much less power; there is never, nor can be, any strengthening of State power without a corresponding and roughly equivalent depletion of social power.

Moreover, it follows that with any exercise of State power, not only the exercise of social power in the same direction, but the disposition to exercise it in that direction, tends to dwindle. Mayor Gaynor astonished the whole of New York when he pointed out to a correspondent who had been complaining about the inefficiency of the police, that any citizen has the right to arrest a malefactor and bring him before a magistrate. "The law of England and of this country," he wrote, "has been very careful to confer no more right in that respect upon policemen and constables than it confers on every citizen." State exercise of that right through a police force had gone on so steadily that not only were citizens indisposed to exercise it, but probably not one in ten thousand knew he had it.

Heretofore in this country sudden crises of misfortune have been met by a mobilization of social power. In fact (except for certain institutional enterprises like the home for the aged, the lunatic-asylum, city-hospital and county-poorhouse) destitution, unemployment, "depression" and similar ills, have been no concern of the State, but have been relieved by the application of social power. Under Mr. Roosevelt, however, the State assumed this function, publicly announcing the doctrine, brand-new in our history, that the State owes its citizens a living. Students of politics, of course, saw in this merely an astute proposal for a prodigious enhancement of State power; merely what, as long ago as 1794, James Madison called "the old trick of turning every contingency into a resource for accumulating force in the government"; and the passage of time has proved that they were right. The effect of this upon the balance between State power and social power is clear, and also its effect of a general indoctrination with the idea that an exercise of social power upon such matters is no longer called for.

It is largely in this way that the progressive conversion of social power into State power

becomes acceptable and gets itself accepted.[1]
When the Johnstown flood occurred, social
power was immediately mobilized and applied with intelligence and vigour. Its abundance, measured by money alone, was so great
that when everything was finally put in order,
something like a million dollars remained.
If such a catastrophe happened now, not only
is social power perhaps too depleted for the
like exercise, but the general instinct would
be to let the State see to it. Not only has
social power atrophied to that extent, but the
disposition to exercise it in that particular direction has atrophied with it. If the State has
made such matters its business, and has confiscated the social power necessary to deal with
them, why, let it deal with them. We can
get some kind of rough measure of this general atrophy by our own disposition when approached by a beggar. Two years ago we
might have been moved to give him something;
today we are moved to refer him to the State's

[1] The result of a questionnaire published in July,
1935, showed 76.8 per cent of the replies favourable
to the idea that it is the State's duty to see that every
person who wants a job shall have one; 20.1 per cent
were against it, and 3.1 per cent were undecided.

relief-agency. The State has said to society, You are either not exercising enough power to meet the emergency, or are exercising it in what I think is an incompetent way, so I shall confiscate your power, and exercise it to suit myself. Hence when a beggar asks us for a quarter, our instinct is to say that the State has already confiscated our quarter for his benefit, and he should go to the State about it.

Every positive intervention that the State makes upon industry and commerce has a similar effect. When the State intervenes to fix wages or prices, or to prescribe the conditions of competition, it virtually tells the enterpriser that he is not exercising social power in the right way, and therefore it proposes to confiscate his power and exercise it according to the State's own judgment of what is best. Hence the enterpriser's instinct is to let the State look after the consequences. As a simple illustration of this, a manufacturer of a highly specialized type of textiles was saying to me the other day that he had kept his mill going at a loss for five years because he did not want to turn his workpeople on the street in such hard times, but now that the State had stepped in to tell him how he must run his business, the State might jolly well take the responsibility.

The process of converting social power into State power may perhaps be seen at its simplest in cases where the State's intervention is directly competitive. The accumulation of State power in various countries has been so accelerated and diversified within the last twenty years that we now see the State functioning as telegraphist, telephonist, match-pedlar, radio-operator, cannon-founder, railway-builder and owner, railway-operator, wholesale and retail tobacconist, shipbuilder and owner, chief chemist, harbour-maker and dockbuilder, housebuilder, chief educator, newspaper-proprietor, food-purveyor, dealer in insurance, and so on through a long list.[2] It

[2] In this country, the State is at present manufacturing furniture, grinding flour, producing fertilizer, building houses; selling farm-products, dairy-products, textiles, canned goods, and electrical apparatus; operating employment-agencies and home-loan offices; financing exports and imports; financing agriculture. It also controls the issuance of securities, communications by wire and radio, discount-rates, oil-production, power-production, commercial competition, the production and sale of alcohol, and the use of inland waterways and railways.

is obvious that private forms of these enterprises must tend to dwindle in proportion as
the energy of the State's encroachments on
them increases, for the competition of social
power with State power is always disadvan-
taged, since the State can arrange the terms of
competition to suit itself, even to the point of
outlawing any exercise of social power whatever in the premises; in other words, giving
itself a monopoly. Instances of this expedient
are common; the one we are probably best
acquainted with is the State's monopoly of
letter-carrying. Social power is estopped by
sheer fiat from application to this form of
enterprise, notwithstanding it could carry it
on far cheaper, and, in this country at least,
far better. The advantages of this monopoly
in promoting the State's interests are peculiar.
No other, probably, could secure so large and
well-distributed a volume of patronage, under
the guise of a public service in constant use
by so large a number of people; it plants a
lieutenant of the State at every country-cross-
road. It is by no means a pure coincidence
that an administration's chief almoner and

whip-at-large is so regularly appointed Post-master-general.

Thus the State "turns every contingency into a resource" for accumulating power in itself, always at the expense of social power; and with this it develops a habit of acquiescence in the people. New generations appear, each temperamentally adjusted—or as I believe our American glossary now has it, "conditioned"— to new increments of State power, and they tend to take the process of continuous accumulation as quite in order. All the State's institutional voices unite in confirming this tendency; they unite in exhibiting the progressive conversion of social power into State power as something not only quite in order, but even as wholesome and necessary for the public good.

II

In the United States at the present time, the principal indexes of the increase of State power are three in number. First, the point to which the centralization of State authority has been carried. Practically all the sovereign rights and powers of the smaller political units—all of them that are significant enough to be worth absorbing—have been absorbed by the federal unit; nor is this all. State power has not only been thus concentrated at Washington, but it has been so far concentrated into the hands of the Executive that the existing régime is a régime of personal government. It is nominally republican, but actually monocratic; a curious anomaly, but highly characteristic of a people little gifted with intellectual integrity. Personal government is not exercised here in the same ways as in Italy, Russia or Germany, for there is as yet no State interest to be served by so doing, but rather the contrary; while in those countries there is. But personal government is always personal government; the mode of its exercise is a matter of immediate political expediency, and is determined entirely by circumstances.

This régime was established by a *coup d'État* of a new and unusual kind, practicable only in a rich country. It was effected, not by violence, like Louis-Napoléon's, or by terrorism, like Mussolini's, but by purchase. It therefore presents what might be called an American variant

of the *coup d'État*.[3]   Our national legislature
was not suppressed by force of arms, like the
French Assembly in 1851, but was bought out
of its functions with public money; and as appeared most conspicuously in the elections of
November, 1934, the consolidation of the *coup
d'État* was effected by the same means; the corresponding functions in the smaller units were
reduced under the personal control of the Executive.[4]   This is a most remarkable phenomenon; possibly nothing quite like it ever
took place; and its character and implications
deserve the most careful attention.

A second index is supplied by the prodigious
extension of the bureaucratic principle that is
now observable.   This is attested *prima facie* by
the number of new boards, bureaux and com-

[3] There is a sort of precedent for it in Roman history, if the story be true in all its details that the
army sold the emperorship to Didius Julianus for
something like five million dollars.   Money has often
been used to grease the wheels of a *coup d'État,* but
straight over-the-counter purchase is unknown, I
think, except in these two instances.

[4] On the day I write this, the newspapers say that
the President is about to order a stoppage on the flow
of federal relief-funds into Louisiana, for the purpose
of bringing Senator Long to terms.   I have seen no
comment, however, on the propriety of this kind of
procedure.

missions set up at Washington in the last two years. They are reported as representing something like 90,000 new employés appointed outside the civil service, and the total of the federal pay-roll in Washington is reported as something over three million dollars per month.[5] This, however, is relatively a small matter. The pressure of centralization has tended powerfully to convert every official and every political aspirant in the smaller units into a venal and complaisant agent of the federal bureaucracy. This presents an interesting parallel with the state of things prevailing in the Roman Empire in the last days of the Flavian dynasty, and afterwards. The rights and practices of local self-government, which were formerly very considerable in the provinces and much more so in the municipalities, were lost by surrender rather than by suppression. The imperial bureaucracy, which up to the second century was comparatively a modest affair, grew rapidly to great size, and local

[5] A friend in the theatrical business tells me that from the box-office point of view, Washington is now the best theatre-town, concert-town and general-amusement town in the United States, far better than New York.

politicians were quick to see the advantage of being on terms with it. They came to Rome with their hats in their hands, as governors, Congressional aspirants and such-like now go to Washington. Their eyes and thoughts were constantly fixed on Rome, because recognition and preferment lay that way; and in their incorrigible sycophancy they became, as Plutarch says, like hypochondriacs who dare not eat or take a bath without consulting their physician.

A third index is seen in the erection of poverty and mendicancy into a permanent political asset. Two years ago, many of our people were in hard straits; to some extent, no doubt, through no fault of their own, though it is now clear that in the popular view of their case, as well as in the political view, the line between the deserving poor and the undeserving poor was not distinctly drawn. Popular feeling ran high at the time, and the prevailing wretchedness was regarded with undiscriminating emotion, as evidence of some general wrong done upon its victims by society at large, rather than as the natural penalty of greed, folly or actual misdoings; which in large part it was. The State, always instinctively "turning every contingency into a resource" for accelerating the conversion of social power into State power, was quick to take advantage of this state of mind. All that was needed to organize these unfortunates into an invaluable political property was to declare the doctrine that the State owes all its citizens a living; and this was accordingly done. It immediately precipitated an enormous mass of subsidized voting-power, an enormous resource for strengthening the State at the expense of society.[6]

III

There is an impression that the enhancement of State power which has taken place since 1932 is provisional and temporary, that the corresponding depletion of social power is by way of a kind of emergency-loan, and therefore is not to be scrutinized too closely. There is every probability that this belief is devoid of

[6] The feature of the approaching campaign of 1936 which will most interest the student of civilization will be the use of the four-billion-dollar relief-fund that has been placed at the President's disposal—the extent, that is, to which it will be distributed on a patronage-basis.

foundation. No doubt our present régime will
be modified in one way and another; indeed,
it must be, for the process of consolidation itself
requires it. But any essential change would be
quite unhistorical, quite without precedent,
and is therefore most unlikely; and by an essential change, I mean one that will tend to redistribute actual power between the State and
society.[7] In the nature of things, there is no
reason why such a change should take place,
and every reason why it should not. We shall
see various apparent recessions, apparent com-
promises, but the one thing we may be quite
sure of is that none of these will tend to diminish actual State power.

For example, we shall no doubt shortly see
the great pressure-group of politically-organized
poverty and mendicancy subsidized indirectly
instead of directly, because State interest can

[7] It must always be kept in mind that there is a
tidal-motion as well as a wave-motion in these matters, and that the wave-motion is of little importance,
relatively. For instance, the Supreme Court's invali-
dation of the National Recovery Act counts for nothing in determining the actual status of personal government. The real question is not how much less the
sum of personal government is now than it was before
that decision, but how much greater it is normally
now than it was in 1932, and in years preceding.

not long keep pace with the hand-over-head disposition of the masses to loot their own Treasury. The method of direct subsidy, or sheer
cash-purchase, will therefore in all probability
soon give way to the indirect method of what
is called "social legislation"; that is, a multiplex
system of State-managed pensions, insurances
and indemnities of various kinds. This is an
apparent recession, and when it occurs it will
no doubt be proclaimed as an actual recession,
no doubt accepted as such; but is it? Does it
actually tend to diminish State power and increase social power? Obviously not, but quite
the opposite. It tends to consolidate firmly this
particular fraction of State power, and opens
the way to getting an indefinite increment upon
it by the mere continuous invention of new
courses and developments of State-administered
social legislation, which is an extremely simple
business. One may add the observation for
whatever its evidential value may be worth,
that if the effect of progressive social legislation
upon the sum-total of State power were unfavourable or even nil, we should hardly have
found Prince de Bismarck and the British Lib-

eral politicians of forty years ago going in for anything remotely resembling it.

When, therefore, the inquiring student of civilization has occasion to observe this or any other apparent recession upon any point of our present régime,[8] he may content himself with asking the one question, *What effect has this upon the sum-total of State power?* The answer he gives himself will show conclusively whether the recession is actual or apparent, and this is all he is concerned to know.

There is also an impression that if actual recessions do not come about of themselves, they may be brought about by the expedient of voting one political party out and another one in. This idea rests upon certain assumptions that experience has shown to be unsound; the first one being that the power of the ballot is what republican political theory makes it out to be, and that therefore the electorate has an effective choice in the matter. It is a matter of open and notorious fact that nothing like this is true. Our nominally republican system is actually built on an imperial model, with our profes-

---

[8] As, for example, the spectacular voiding of the National Recovery Act.

sional politicians standing in the place of the
prætorian guards; they meet from time to time,
decide what can be "got away with," and how,
and who is to do it; and the electorate votes according to their prescriptions.   Under these
conditions it is easy to provide the appearance
of any desired concession of State power, without the reality; our history shows innumerable
instances of very easy dealing with problems in
practical politics much more difficult than that.
One may remark in this connexion also the notoriously baseless assumption that party-desig-
nations connote principles, and that party-
pledges imply performance.   Moreover, underlying these assumptions and all others that faith
in "political action" contemplates, is the assumption that the interests of the State and the
interests of society are, at least theoretically,
identical; whereas in theory they are directly
opposed, and this opposition invariably declares
itself in practice to the precise extent that circumstances permit.

However, without pursuing these matters
further at the moment, it is probably enough
to observe here that in the nature of things the
exercise of personal government, the control of

a huge and growing bureaucracy, and the management of an enormous mass of subsidized
voting-power, are as agreeable to one stripe of
politician as they are to another. Presumably
they interest a Republican or a Progressive as
much as they do a Democrat, Communist,
Farmer-Labourite, Socialist, or whatever a politician may, for electioneering purposes, see fit
to call himself. This was demonstrated in the
local campaigns of 1934 by the practical attitude of politicians who represented nominal
opposition parties. It is now being further
demonstrated by the derisible haste that the
leaders of the official opposition are making
towards what they call "reorganization" of their
party. One may well be inattentive to their
words; their actions, however, mean simply
that the recent accretions of State power are
here to stay, and that they are aware of it; and
that, such being the case, they are preparing to
dispose themselves most advantageously in a
contest for their control and management.
This is all that "reorganization" of the Republican party means, and all it is meant to mean;
and this is in itself quite enough to show that
any expectation of an essential change of régime

through a change of party-administration is illusory. On the contrary, it is clear that whatever party-competition we shall see hereafter will be on the same terms as heretofore. It will be a competition for control and management, and it would naturally issue in still closer centralization, still further extension of the bureaucratic principle, and still larger concessions to subsidized voting-power. This course would be strictly historical, and is furthermore to be expected as lying in the nature of things, as it so obviously does.

Indeed, it is by this means that the aim of the collectivists seems likeliest to be attained in this country; this aim being the complete extinction of social power through absorption by the State. Their fundamental doctrine was formulated and invested with a quasi-religious sanction by the idealist philosophers of the last century; and among peoples who have accepted it in terms as well as in fact, it is expressed in formulas almost identical with theirs. Thus, for example, when Hitler says that "the State dominates the nation because it alone represents it," he is only putting into loose popular language the formula of Hegel, that "the State is the general substance, whereof individuals are but accidents." Or, again, when Mussolini says, "Everything for the State; nothing outside the State; nothing against the State," he is merely vulgarizing the doctrine of Fichte, that "the State is the superior power, ultimate and beyond appeal, absolutely independent."

It may be in place to remark here the essential identity of the various extant forms of collectivism. The superficial distinctions of Fascism, Bolshevism, Hitlerism, are the concern of journalists and publicists; the serious student [9] sees in them only the one root-idea of a complete conversion of social power into State power. When Hitler and Mussolini invoke a kind of debased and hoodwinking mysticism to aid their acceleration of this process, the student at once recognizes his old friend, the formula of Hegel, that "the State incarnates the Divine Idea upon earth," and he is not hoodwinked. The journalist and the impression-

[9] This book is a sort of syllabus or précis of some lectures to students of American history and politics —mostly graduate students—and it therefore presupposes some little acquaintance with those subjects. The few references I have given, however, will put any reader in the way of documenting and amplifying it satisfactorily.

able traveller may make what they will of "the new religion of Bolshevism"; the student contents himself with remarking clearly the exact nature of the process which this inculcation is designed to sanction.

IV

This process—the conversion of social power into State power—has not been carried as far here as it has elsewhere; as it has in Russia, Italy or Germany, for example. Two things, however, are to be observed. First, that it has gone a long way, at a rate of progress which has of late been greatly accelerated. What has chiefly differentiated its progress here from its progress in other countries is its unspectacular character. Mr. Jefferson wrote in 1823 that there was no danger he dreaded so much as "the consolidation [i.e., centralization] of our government by the noiseless and therefore unalarming instrumentality of the Supreme Court." These words characterize every advance that we have made in State aggrandizement. Each one has been noiseless and therefore unalarming, especially to a people notoriously preoccupied, inattentive

and incurious. Even the *coup d'État* of 1932
was noiseless and unalarming. In Russia, Italy,
Germany, the *coup d'État* was violent and spectacular; it had to be; but here it was neither.
Under cover of a nation-wide, State-managed
mobilization of inane buffoonery and aimless
commotion, it took place in so unspectacular a
way that its true nature escaped notice, and
even now is not generally understood. The
method of consolidating the ensuing régime,
moreover, was also noiseless and unalarming;
it was merely the prosaic and unspectacular
"higgling of the market," to which a long and
uniform political experience had accustomed
us. A visitor from a poorer and thriftier country might have regarded Mr. Farley's activities
in the local campaigns of 1934 as striking or
even spectacular, but they made no such impression on us. They seemed so familiar, so
much the regular thing, that one heard little
comment on them. Moreover, political habit
led us to attribute whatever unfavourable comment we did hear, to interest; either partisan or
monetary interest, or both. We put it down
as the jaundiced judgment of persons with axes

to grind; and naturally the régime did all it could to encourage this view.

The second thing to be observed is that certain formulas, certain arrangements of words, stand as an obstacle in the way of our perceiving how far the conversion of social power into State power has actually gone. The force of phrase and name distorts the identification of our own actual acceptances and acquiescences. We are accustomed to the rehearsal of certain poetic litanies, and provided their cadence be kept entire, we are indifferent to their correspondence with truth and fact. When Hegel's doctrine of the State, for example, is restated in terms by Hitler and Mussolini, it is distinctly offensive to us, and we congratulate ourselves on our freedom from the "yoke of a dictator's tyranny." No American politician would dream of breaking in on our routine of litanies with anything of the kind. We may imagine, for example, the shock to popular sentiment that would ensue upon Mr. Roosevelt's declaring publicly that "the State embraces everything, and nothing has value outside the State. The State creates right." Yet an American politician, as long as he does not formulate that

doctrine in set terms, may go further with it
in a practical way than Mussolini has gone, and
without trouble or question. Suppose Mr.
Roosevelt should defend his régime by publicly
reasserting Hegel's dictum that "the State alone
possesses rights, because it is the strongest."
One can hardly imagine that our public would
get that down without a great deal of retching.
Yet how far, really, is that doctrine alien to our
public's actual acquiescences? Surely not far.

The point is that in respect of the relation
between the theory and the actual practice of
public affairs, the American is the most un-
philosophical of beings. The rationalization of
conduct in general is most repugnant to him;
he prefers to emotionalize it. He is indifferent
to the theory of things, so long as he may re-
hearse his formulas; and so long as he can listen
to the patter of his litanies, no practical inconsistency disturbs him—indeed, he gives no evidence of even recognizing it as an inconsistency.

The ablest and most acute observer among
the many who came from Europe to look us
over in the early part of the last century was the
one who is for some reason the most neglected,
notwithstanding that in our present circum-

stances, especially, he is worth more to us than all the de Tocquevilles, Bryces, Trollopes and Chateaubriands put together. This was the noted St.-Simonien and political economist, Michel Chevalier. Professor Chinard, in his admirable biographical study of John Adams, has called attention to Chevalier's observation that the American people have "the morale of an army on the march." The more one thinks of this, the more clearly one sees how little there is in what our publicists are fond of calling "the American psychology" that it does not exactly account for; and it exactly accounts for the trait that we are considering.

An army on the march has no philosophy; it views itself as a creature of the moment. It does not rationalize conduct except in terms of an immediate end. As Tennyson observed, there is a pretty strict official understanding against its doing so; "theirs not to reason why." Emotionalizing conduct is another matter, and the more of it the better; it is encouraged by a whole elaborate paraphernalia of showy etiquette, flags, music, uniforms, decorations, and the careful cultivation of a very special sort of comradery. In every relation to "the reason of

the thing," however—in the ability and eagerness, as Plato puts it, "to see things as they are"
—the mentality of an army on the march is
merely so much delayed adolescence; it remains
persistently, incorrigibly and notoriously infantile.

Past generations of Americans, as Martin
Chuzzlewit left record, erected this infantilism
into a distinguishing virtue, and they took great
pride in it as the mark of a chosen people, destined to live forever amidst the glory of their
own unparalleled achievements *wie Gott in
Frankreich.* Mr. Jefferson Brick, General
Choke and the Honourable Elijah Pogram
made a first-class job of indoctrinating their
countrymen with the idea that a philosophy is
wholly unnecessary, and that a concern with
the theory of things is effeminate and unbecom-
ing. An envious and presumably dissolute
Frenchman may say what he likes about the
morale of an army on the march, but the fact
remains that it has brought us where we are,
and has got us what we have. Look at a con-
tinent subdued, see the spread of our industry
and commerce, our railways, newspapers, fi-
nance-companies, schools, colleges, what you

will! Well, if all this has been done without a philosophy, if we have grown to this unrivalled greatness without any attention to the theory of things, does it not show that philosophy and the theory of things are all moonshine, and not worth a practical people's consideration? The morale of an army on the march is good enough for us, and we are proud of it.

The present generation does not speak in quite this tone of robust certitude. It seems, if anything, rather less openly contemptuous of philosophy; one even sees some signs of a suspicion that in our present circumstances the theory of things might be worth looking into, and it is especially towards the theory of sovereignty and rulership that this new attitude of hospitality appears to be developing. The condition of public affairs in all countries, notably in our own, has done more than bring under review the mere current practice of politics, the character and quality of representative politicians, and the relative merits of this-or-that form or mode of government. It has served to suggest attention to the one institution whereof all these forms or modes are but the several, and, from the theoretical point of view, indif-

ferent, manifestations. It suggests that finality
does not lie with consideration of species, but
of genus; it does not lie with consideration of
the characteristic marks that differentiate the
republican State, monocratic State, constitutional, collectivist, totalitarian, Hitlerian, Bolshevist, what you will. It lies with consideration of the State itself.

V

There appears to be a curious difficulty about
exercising reflective thought upon the actual
nature of an institution into which one was
born and one's ancestors were born. One ac-
cepts it as one does the atmosphere; one's practical adjustments to it are made by a kind of
reflex. One seldom thinks about the air until
one notices some change, favourable or unfavourable, and then one's thought about it is
special; one thinks about purer air, lighter air,
heavier air, not about air. So it is with certain
human institutions. We know that they exist,
that they affect us in various ways, but we do
not ask how they came to exist, or what their
original intention was, or what primary func-

tion it is that they are actually fulfilling; and
when they affect us so unfavourably that we
rebel against them, we contemplate substituting
nothing beyond some modification or variant of
the same institution. Thus colonial America,
oppressed by the monarchical State, brings in
the republican State; Germany gives up the republican State for the Hitlerian State; Russia
exchanges the monocratic State for the collectivist State; Italy exchanges the constitutionalist State for the "totalitarian" State.

It is interesting to observe that in the year
1935 the average individual's incurious attitude
towards the phenomenon of the State is precisely what his attitude was towards the phenomenon of the Church in the year, say, 1500.
The State was then a very weak institution;
the Church was very strong. The individual
was born into the Church, as his ancestors had
been for generations, in precisely the formal,
documented fashion in which he is now born
into the State. He was taxed for the Church's
support, as he now is for the State's support.
He was supposed to accept the official theory
and doctrine of the Church, to conform to its
discipline, and in a general way to do as it told

him; again, precisely the sanctions that the
State now lays upon him. If he were reluctant
or recalcitrant, the Church made a satisfactory
amount of trouble for him, as the State now
does. Notwithstanding all this, it does not appear to have occurred to the Church-citizen of
that day, any more than it occurs to the State-
citizen of the present, to ask what sort of institution it was that claimed his allegiance.
There it was; he accepted its own account of
itself, took it as it stood, and at its own valuation. Even when he revolted, fifty years later,
he merely exchanged one form or mode of the
Church for another, the Roman for the Calvinist, Lutheran, Zuinglian, or what not; again,
quite as the modern State-citizen exchanges one
mode of the State for another. He did not examine the institution itself, nor does the State-
citizen today.

My purpose in writing is to raise the question
whether the enormous depletion of social
power which we are witnessing everywhere does
not suggest the importance of knowing more
than we do about the essential nature of the
institution that is so rapidly absorbing this

volume of power.[10] One of my friends said to me lately that if the public-utility corporations did not mend their ways, the State would take over their business and operate it. He spoke with a curiously reverent air of finality. Just so, I thought, might a Church-citizen, at the end of the fifteenth century, have spoken of some impending intervention of the Church; and I wondered then whether he had any better-informed and closer-reasoned theory of the State than his prototype had of the Church. Frankly, I am sure he had not. His pseudo-conception was merely an unreasoned acceptance of the State on its own terms and at its own valuation; and in this acceptance he showed himself no more intelligent, and no less, than the whole mass of State-citizenry at large.

It appears to me that with the depletion of social power going on at the rate it is, the State-citizen should look very closely into the essential nature of the institution that is bringing it about. He should ask himself whether he has

[10] An inadequate and partial idea of what this volume amounts to, may be got from the fact that the American State's income from taxation is now about one-third of the nation's total income! This takes into account all forms of taxation, direct and indirect, local and federal.

a theory of the State, and if so, whether he can assure himself that history supports it. He will not find this a matter that can be settled off-hand; it needs a good deal of investigation, and a stiff exercise of reflective thought. He should ask, in the first place, how the State originated, and why; it must have come about somehow, and for some purpose. This seems an extremely easy question to answer, but he will not find it so. Then he should ask what it is that history exhibits continuously as the State's primary function. Then, whether he finds that "the State" and "government" are strictly synonymous terms; he uses them as such, but are they? Are there any invariable characteristic marks that differentiate the institution of government from the institution of the State? Then finally he should decide whether, by the testimony of history, the State is to be regarded as, in essence, a social or an anti-social institution?

It is pretty clear now that if the Church-citizen of 1500 had put his mind on questions as fundamental as these, his civilization might have had a much easier and pleasanter course to run; and the State-citizen of today may profit by his experience.

2

As far back as one can follow the run of civilization, it presents two fundamentally different types of political organization. This difference is not one of degree, but of kind. It does not do to take the one type as merely marking a lower order of civilization and the other a higher; they are commonly so taken, but erroneously. Still less does it do to classify both as species of the same genus—to classify both under the generic name of "government," though this also, until very lately, has always been done, and has always led to confusion and misunderstanding.

A good example of this error and its effects is supplied by Thomas Paine. At the outset of his pamphlet called *Common Sense*, Paine draws a distinction between society and government. While society in any state is a blessing, he says, "government, even in its best state, is but a necessary evil; in its worst state, an in-

tolerable one." In another place, he speaks of
government as "a mode rendered necessary by
the inability of moral virtue to govern the
world." He proceeds then to show how and
why government comes into being. Its origin
is in the common understanding and common
agreement of society; and "the design and end
of government," he says, is "freedom and security." Teleologically, government implements
the common desire of society, first, for freedom,
and second, for security. Beyond this it does
not go; it contemplates no positive intervention
upon the individual, but only a negative intervention. It would seem that in Paine's view
the code of government should be that of the
legendary king Pausole, who prescribed but two
laws for his subjects, the first being, *Hurt no
man,* and the second, *Then do as you please;*
and that the whole business of government
should be the purely negative one of seeing
that this code is carried out.

So far, Paine is sound as he is simple. He
goes on, however, to attack the British political
organization in terms that are logically incon-
clusive. There should be no complaint of this,
for he was writing as a pamphleteer, a special

pleader with an *ad captandum* argument to make, and as everyone knows, he did it most successfully. Nevertheless, the point remains that when he talks about the British system he is talking about a type of political organization essentially different from the type that he has just been describing; different in origin, in intention, in primary function, in the order of interest that it reflects. It did not originate in the common understanding and agreement of society; it originated in conquest and confiscation.[1] Its intention, far from contemplating "freedom and security," contemplated nothing of the kind. It contemplated primarily the continuous economic exploitation of one class by another, and it concerned itself with only so much freedom and security as was consistent with this primary intention; and this was, in fact, very little. Its primary function or exercise was not by way of Paine's purely negative interventions upon the individual, but by

[1] Paine was of course well aware of this. He says, "A French bastard, landing with an armed banditti, and establishing himself king of England against the consent of the natives, is in plain terms a very paltry rascally original." He does not press the point, however, nor in view of his purpose should he be expected to do so.

way of innumerable and most onerous positive interventions, all of which were for the purpose of maintaining the stratification of society into an owning and exploiting class, and a property-less dependent class. The order of interest that it reflected was not social, but purely anti-social; and those who administered it, judged by the common standard of ethics, or even the common standard of law as applied to private persons, were indistinguishable from a professional-criminal class.

Clearly, then, we have two distinct types of political organization to take into account; and clearly, too, when their origins are considered, it is impossible to make out that the one is a mere perversion of the other. Therefore, when we include both types under a general term like *government,* we get into logical difficulties; difficulties of which most writers on the subject have been more or less vaguely aware, but which, until within the last half-century, none of them has tried to resolve.

Mr. Jefferson, for example, remarked that the hunting tribes of Indians, with which he had a good deal to do in his early days, had a highly organized and admirable social order, but were "without government." Commenting on this, he wrote Madison that "it is a problem not clear in my mind that [this] condition is not the best," but he suspected that it was "inconsistent with any great degree of population." Schoolcraft observes that the Chippewas, though living in a highly-organized social order, had no "regular" government. Herbert Spencer, speaking of the Bechuanas, Araucanians and Koranna Hottentots, says they have no "definite" government; while Parkman, in his introduction to *The Conspiracy of Pontiac,* reports the same phenomenon, and is frankly puzzled by its apparent anomalies.

Paine's theory of government agrees exactly with the theory set forth by Mr. Jefferson in the Declaration of Independence. The doctrine of natural rights, which is explicit in the Declaration, is implicit in *Common Sense;* [2] and Paine's view of the "design and end of government" is precisely the Declaration's view, that "to secure these rights, governments

[2] In *Rights of Man,* Paine is as explicit about this doctrine as the Declaration is; and in several places throughout his pamphlets, he asserts that all civil rights are founded on natural rights, and proceed from them.

are instituted among men"; and further,
Paine's view of the origin of government is that
it "derives its just powers from the consent of
the governed." Now, if we apply Paine's formulas or the Declaration's formulas, it is
abundantly clear that the Virginian Indians
had government; Mr. Jefferson's own observations show that they had it. Their political
organization, simple as it was, answered its purpose. Their code-apparatus sufficed for assur-
ing freedom and security to the individual, and
for dealing with such trespasses as in that state
of society the individual might encounter—
fraud, theft, assault, adultery, murder. The
same is as clearly true of the various peoples
cited by Parkman, Schoolcraft and Spencer.
Assuredly, if the language of the Declaration
amounts to anything, all these peoples had government; and all these reporters make it appear
as a government quite competent to its purpose.

Therefore when Mr. Jefferson says his Indians were "without government," he must be
taken to mean that they did not have a type of
government like the one he knew; and when
Schoolcraft and Spencer speak of "regular" and
"definite" government, their qualifying words

must be taken in the same way. This type of government, nevertheless, has always existed and still exists, answering perfectly to Paine's formulas and the Declaration's formulas; though it is a type which we also, most of us, have seldom had the chance to observe. It may not be put down as the mark of an inferior race, for institutional simplicity is in itself by no means a mark of backwardness or inferiority; and it has been sufficiently shown that in certain essential respects the peoples who have this type of government are, by comparison, in a position to say a good deal for themselves on the score of a civilized character. Mr. Jefferson's own testimony on this point is worth notice, and so is Parkman's. This type, however, even though documented by the Declaration, is fundamentally so different from the type that has always prevailed in history, and is still prevailing in the world at the moment, that for the sake of clearness the two types should be set apart by name, as they are by nature. They are so different in theory that drawing a sharp distinction between them is now probably the most important duty that civilization owes to its own safety. Hence it is by no means either an arbitrary or academic proceeding to give the one type the name of *government,* and to call the second type simply *the State.*

II

Aristotle, confusing the idea of the State with the idea of government, thought the State originated out of the natural grouping of the family. Other Greek philosophers, labouring under the same confusion, somewhat anticipated Rousseau in finding its origin in the social nature and disposition of the individual; while an opposing school, which held that the individual is naturally anti-social, more or less anticipated Hobbes by finding it in an enforced compromise among the anti-social tendencies of individuals. Another view, implicit in the doctrine of Adam Smith, is that the State originated in the association of certain individuals who showed a marked superiority in the economic virtues of diligence, prudence and thrift. The idealist philosophers, variously applying Kant's transcendentalism to the problem, came to still different conclusions; and one or two other views, rather less plausible, perhaps, than any of the foregoing, have been advanced.

The root-trouble with all these views is not precisely that they are conjectural, but that they are based on incompetent observation. They miss the invariable characteristic marks that the subject presents; as, for example, until quite lately, all views of the origin of malaria missed the invariable ministrations of the mosquito, or as opinions about the bubonic plague missed the invariable mark of the rat-parasite. It is only within the last half-century that the historical method has been applied to the problem of the State.[3] This method runs back the phenomenon of the State to its first appearance in documented history, observing its invariable characteristic marks, and drawing inferences as

[3] By Gumplowicz, professor at Graz, and after him, by Oppenheimer, professor of politics at Frankfort. I have followed them throughout this section. The findings of these Galileos are so damaging to the prestige that the State has everywhere built up for itself that professional authority in general has been very circumspect about approaching them, naturally preferring to give them a wide berth; but in the long-run, this is a small matter. Honourable and distinguished exceptions appear in Vierkandt, Wilhelm Wundt, and the revered patriarch of German economic studies, Adolf Wagner.

indicated. There are so many clear intimations of this method in earlier writers—one finds them as far back as Strabo—that one wonders why its systematic application was so long deferred; but in all such cases, as with malaria and typhus, when the characteristic mark is once determined, it is so obvious that one always wonders why it was so long unnoticed. Perhaps in the case of the State, the best one can say is that the coöperation of the *Zeitgeist* was necessary, and that it could be had no sooner.

The positive testimony of history is that the State invariably had its origin in conquest and confiscation. No primitive State known to history originated in any other manner.[4] On the negative side, it has been proved beyond peradventure that no primitive State could possibly have had any other origin.[5] Moreover, the sole

[4] An excellent example of primitive practice, effected by modern technique, is furnished by the new State of Manchoukuo, and another bids fair to be furnished in consequence of the Italian State's operations in Ethiopia.

[5] The mathematics of this demonstration are extremely interesting. A résumé of them is given in Oppenheimer's treatise *Der Staat*, ch. I, and they are worked out in full in his *Theorie der Reinen und Politischen Oekonomie*.

invariable characteristic of the State is the economic exploitation of one class by another. In this sense, every State known to history is a class-State. Oppenheimer defines the State, in respect of its origin, as an institution "forced on a defeated group by a conquering group, with a view only to systematizing the domination of the conquered by the conquerors, and safeguarding itself against insurrection from within and attack from without. This domination had no other final purpose than the economic exploitation of the conquered group by the victorious group."

An American statesman, John Jay, accomplished the respectable feat of compressing the whole doctrine of conquest into a single sentence. "Nations in general," he said, "will go to war whenever there is a prospect of getting something by it." Any considerable economic accumulation, or any considerable body of natural resources, is an incentive to conquest. The primitive technique was that of raiding the coveted possessions, appropriating them entire, and either exterminating the possessors, or dispersing them beyond convenient reach. Very early, however, it was seen to be in gen-

eral more profitable to reduce the possessors to
dependence, and use them as labour-motors;
and the primitive technique was accordingly
modified. Under special circumstances, where
this exploitation was either impracticable or
unprofitable, the primitive technique is even
now occasionally revived, as by the Spaniards in
South America, or by ourselves against the
Indians. But these circumstances are excep-
tional; the modified technique has been in use
almost from the beginning, and everywhere its
first appearance marks the origin of the State.
Citing Ranke's observations on the technique
of the raiding herdsmen, the Hyksos, who established their State in Egypt about B.C. 2000,
Gumplowicz remarks that Ranke's words very
well sum up the political history of mankind.

Indeed, the modified technique never varies.
"Everywhere we see a militant group of fierce
men forcing the frontier of some more peace-
able people, settling down upon them and establishing the State, with themselves as an aris-
tocracy. In Mesopotamia, irruption succeeds
irruption, State succeeds State, Babylonians,
Amoritans, Assyrians, Arabs, Medes, Persians,
Macedonians, Parthians, Mongols, Seldshuks,

Tatars, Turks; in the Nile valley, Hyksos, Nubians, Persians, Greeks, Romans, Arabs, Turks; in Greece, the Doric States are specific examples; in Italy, Romans, Ostrogoths, Lombards, Franks, Germans; in Spain, Carthaginians, Visigoths, Arabs; in Gaul, Romans, Franks, Burgundians, Normans; in Britain, Saxons, Normans." Everywhere we find the political organization proceeding from the same origin, and presenting the same mark of intention, namely: the economic exploitation of a defeated group by a conquering group.

Everywhere, that is, with but the one significant exception. Wherever economic exploitation has been for any reason either impracticable or unprofitable, the State has never come into existence; government has existed, but the State, never. The American hunting tribes, for example, whose organization so puzzled our observers, never formed a State, for there is no way to reduce a hunter to economic dependence and make him hunt for you.[6] Con-

---

[6] Except, of course, by preëmption of the land under the State-system of tenure, but for occupational reasons this would not be worth a hunting tribe's attempting. Bicknell, the historian of Rhode Island, suggests that the troubles over Indian treaties arose

quest and confiscation were no doubt practicable, but no economic gain would be got by
it, for confiscation would give the aggressors
but little beyond what they already had; the
most that could come of it would be the satisfaction of some sort of feud. For like reasons
primitive peasants never formed a State. The
economic accumulations of their neighbours
were too slight and too perishable to be interesting; [7] and especially with the abundance of
free land about, the enslavement of their
neighbours would be impracticable, if only for
the police-problems involved.[8]

from the fact that the Indians did not understand the
State-system of land-tenure, never having had anything like it; their understanding was that the whites
were admitted only to the same communal use of
land that they themselves enjoyed. It is interesting
to remark that the settled fishing tribes of the North-
west formed a State. Their occupation made economic exploitation both practicable and profitable,
and they resorted to conquest and confiscation to introduce it.

[7] It is strange that so little attention has been paid
to the singular immunity enjoyed by certain small
and poor peoples amidst great collisions of State interest. Throughout the late war, for example, Swit-
zerland, which has nothing worth stealing, was never
raided or disturbed.

[8] Marx's chapter on colonization is interesting in
this connexion, especially for his observation that

It may now be easily seen how great the difference is between the institution of government, as understood by Paine and the Declaration of Independence, and the institution of the State. Government may quite conceivably have originated as Paine thought it did, or Aristotle, or Hobbes, or Rousseau; whereas the State not only never did originate in any of those ways, but never could have done so. The nature and intention of government, as adduced by Parkman, Schoolcraft and Spencer, are social. Based on the idea of natural rights, government secures those rights to the individual by strictly negative intervention, making justice costless and easy of access; and beyond that it does not go. The State, on the other hand, both in its genesis and by its primary intention, is purely anti-social. It is not based on the idea of natural rights, but on the idea that the individual has no rights except those

economic exploitation is impracticable until expropriation from the land has taken place. Here he is in full agreement with the whole line of fundamental economists, from Turgôt, Franklin and John Taylor down to Theodor Hertzka and Henry George. Marx, however, apparently did not see that his observation left him with something of a problem on his hands, for he does little more with it than record the fact.

that the State may provisionally grant him. It has always made justice costly and difficult of access, and has invariably held itself above justice and common morality whenever it could advantage itself by so doing.[9] So far from encouraging a wholesome development of social power, it has invariably, as Madison said, turned every contingency into a resource for depleting social power and enhancing State power.[10] As Dr. Sigmund Freud has observed, it can not even be said that the State has ever shown any disposition to suppress crime, but only to safeguard its own monopoly of crime. In Russia and Germany, for example, we have lately seen the State moving with great alacrity against infringement of its monopoly by private persons, while at the same time exercising that monopoly with unconscionable ruthlessness. Taking the State wherever found, striking into its history at any point, one sees no way to differentiate the activities of its founders, administrators and beneficiaries from those of a professional-criminal class.

[9] John Bright said he had known the British Parliament to do some good things, but never knew it to do a good thing merely because it was a good thing.
[10] *Reflections*, I.

III

Such are the antecedents of the institution which is everywhere now so busily converting social power by wholesale into State power.[11] The recognition of them goes a long way towards resolving most, if not all, of the apparent anomalies which the conduct of the modern State exhibits. It is of great help, for example, in accounting for the open and notorious fact that the State always moves slowly and grudgingly towards any purpose that accrues to society's advantage, but moves rapidly and with alacrity towards one that accrues to its own advantage; nor does it ever move towards social purposes on its own initiative,

[11] In this country the condition of several socially-valuable industries seems at the moment to be a pretty fair index of this process. The State's positive interventions have so far depleted social power that by all accounts these particular applications of it are on the verge of being no longer practicable. In Italy, the State now absorbs fifty per cent of the total national income. Italy appears to be rehearsing her ancient history in something more than a sentimental fashion, for by the end of the second century social power had been so largely transmuted into State power that nobody could do any business at all. There was not enough social power left to pay the State's bills.

but only under heavy pressure, while its motion towards anti-social purposes is self-sprung.

Englishmen of the last century remarked this
fact with justifiable anxiety, as they watched the
rapid depletion of social power by the British
State. One of them was Herbert Spencer, who
published a series of essays which were subsequently put together in a volume called *The
Man versus the State*. With our public affairs
in the shape they are, it is rather remarkable
that no American publicist has improved the
chance to reproduce these essays verbatim,
merely substituting illustrations drawn from
American history for those which Spencer draws
from English history. If this were properly
done, it would make one of the most pertinent
and useful works that could be produced at
this time.[12]

[12] It seems a most discreditable thing that this century has not seen produced in America an intellectually respectable presentation of the complete case
against the State's progressive confiscations of social
power; a presentation, that is, which bears the mark
of having sound history and a sound philosophy behind it. Mere interested touting of "rugged individualism" and agonized fustian about the constitution are so specious, so frankly unscrupulous, that
they have become contemptible. Consequently collectivism has easily had all the best of it, intellec-

These essays are devoted to examining the several aspects of the contemporary growth of State power in England. In the essay called *Over-legislation,* Spencer remarks the fact so notoriously common in our experience,[13] that when State power is applied to social purposes, its action is invariably "slow, stupid, extravagant, unadaptive, corrupt and obstructive." He devotes several paragraphs to each count, assembling a complete array of proof. When he ends, discussion ends; there is simply nothing to be said. He shows further that the State does not even fulfil efficiently what he calls its

tually, and the results are now apparent. Collectivism has even succeeded in foisting its glossary of arbitrary definitions upon us; we all speak of our economic system, for instance, as "capitalist," when there has never been a system, nor can one be imagined, that is not capitalist. By contrast, when British collectivism undertook to deal, say with Lecky, Bagehot, Professor Huxley and Herbert Spencer, it got full change for its money. Whatever steps Britain has taken towards collectivism, or may take, it at least has had all the chance in the world to know precisely where it was going, which we have not had.

[13] Yesterday I passed over a short stretch of new road built by State power, applied through one of the grotesque alphabetical tentacles of our bureaucracy. It cost $87,348.56. Social power, represented by a contractor's figure in competitive bidding, would have built it for $38,668.20, a difference, roughly, of one hundred per cent!

"unquestionable duties" to society; it does not efficiently adjudge and defend the individual's elemental rights. This being so—and with us this too is a matter of notoriously common experience—Spencer sees no reason to expect that State power will be more efficiently applied to secondary social purposes. "Had we, in short, proved its efficiency as judge and defender, instead of having found it treacherous, cruel, and anxiously to be shunned, there would be some encouragement to hope other benefits at its hands."

Yet, he remarks, it is just this monstrously extravagant hope that society is continually indulging; and indulging in the face of daily evidence that it is illusory. He points to the anomaly which we have all noticed as so regularly presented by newspapers. Take up one, says Spencer, and you will probably find a leading editorial "exposing the corruption, negligence or mismanagement of some State department. Cast your eye down the next column, and it is not unlikely that you will read proposals for an extension of State supervision.[14]

[14] All the newspaper-comments that I have read concerning the recent marine disasters that befell the

. . . Thus while every day chronicles a failure, there every day reappears the belief that it needs but an Act of Parliament and a staff of officers to effect any end desired.[15]   Nowhere is the perennial faith of mankind better seen."

It is unnecessary to say that the reasons which Spencer gives for the anti-social behaviour of the State are abundantly valid, but we may now see how powerfully they are reinforced by the findings of the historical method; a method which had not been applied when Spencer wrote.   These findings being what they are, it is manifest that the conduct which Spencer complains of is strictly historical.   When the town-dwelling merchants of the eighteenth century displaced the landholding nobility in control of the State's mechanism, they did not change the State's character; they merely adapted its mechanism to their own special interests, and strengthened it immeasurably.[16]

Ward Line have, without exception, led up to just such proposals!

[15] Our recent experiences with prohibition might be thought to have suggested this belief as fatuous, but apparently they have not done so.

[16] This point is well discussed by the Spanish philosopher Ortega y Gasset, *The Revolt of the Masses*, ch. XIII (English translation), in which he does not

The merchant-State remained an anti-social institution, a pure class-State, like the State of the
nobility; its intention and function remained
unchanged, save for the adaptations necessary
to suit the new order of interests that it was
thenceforth to serve. Therefore in its flagrant
disservice of social purposes, for which Spencer
arraigns it, the State was acting strictly in character.

Spencer does not discuss what he calls "the
perennial faith of mankind" in State action, but
contents himself with elaborating the senten-
tious observation of Guizot, that "a belief in
the sovereign power of political machinery" is
nothing less than "a gross delusion." This faith
is chiefly an effect of the immense prestige

scruple to say that the State's rapid depletion of social
power is "the greatest danger that today threatens
civilization." He also gives a good idea of what may
be expected when a third, economically-composite,
class in turn takes over the mechanism of the State,
as the merchant class took it over from the nobility.
Surely no better forecast could be made of what is
taking place in this country at the moment, than this:
"The mass-man does in fact believe that he is the
State, and he will tend more and more to set its machinery working, on whatsoever pretext, to crush beneath it any creative minority which disturbs it—disturbs it in any order of things; in politics, in ideas,
in industry."

which the State has diligently built up for itself in the century or more since the doctrine of *jure divino* rulership gave way. We need not consider the various instruments that the State employs in building up its prestige; most of them are well known, and their uses well understood. There is one, however, which is in a sense peculiar to the republican State. Republicanism permits the individual to persuade himself that the State is his creation, that State action is his action, that when it expresses itself it expresses him, and when it is glorified he is glorified. The republican State encourages this persuasion with all its power, aware that it is the most efficient instrument for enhancing its own prestige. Lincoln's phrase, "of the people, by the people, for the people" was probably the most effective single stroke of propaganda ever made in behalf of republican State prestige.

Thus the individual's sense of his own importance inclines him strongly to resent the suggestion that the State is by nature anti-social. He looks on its failures and misfeasances with somewhat the eye of a parent, giving it the benefit of a special code of ethics. Moreover, he has always the expectation that the State will learn by its mistakes, and do better. Granting that its technique with social purposes is blundering, wasteful and vicious—even admitting, with the public official whom Spencer cites, that wherever the State is, there is villainy—he sees no reason why, with an increase of experience and responsibility, the State should not improve.

Something like this appears to be the basic assumption of collectivism. Let but the State confiscate *all* social power, and its interests will become identical with those of society. Granting that the State is of anti-social origin, and that it has borne a uniformly anti-social character throughout its history, let it but extinguish social power completely, and its character will change; it will merge with society, and thereby become society's efficient and disinterested organ. The historic State, in short, will disappear, and government only will remain. It is an attractive idea; the hope of its being somehow translated into practice is what, only so few years ago, made "the Russian experiment" so irresistibly fascinating to generous spirits who felt themselves hopelessly State-ridden. A closer examination of the State's activities, however, will show that this idea, attractive though it be, goes to pieces against the iron law of fundamental economics, that *man tends always to satisfy his needs and desires with the least possible exertion.* Let us see how this is so.

IV

There are two methods, or means, and only two, whereby man's needs and desires can be satisfied. One is the production and exchange of wealth; this is the *economic means.*[17] The other is the uncompensated appropriation of wealth produced by others; this is the *political means.* The primitive exercise of the political means was, as we have seen, by conquest, confiscation, expropriation, and the introduction of a slave-economy. The conqueror parcelled out the conquered territory among beneficiaries, who thenceforth satisfied their needs and desires by exploiting the labour of the enslaved inhabitants.[18] The feudal State, and the mer-

[17] Oppenheimer, *Der Staat,* ch. I. Services are also, of course, a subject of economic exchange.

[18] In America, where the native huntsmen were not exploitable, the beneficiaries—the Virginia Company,

chant-State, wherever found, merely took over
and developed successively the heritage of character, intention and apparatus of exploitation
which the primitive State transmitted to them;
they are in essence merely higher integrations
of the primitive State.

The State, then, whether primitive, feudal or
merchant, is *the organization of the political
means*. Now, since man tends always to satisfy
his needs and desires with the least possible
exertion, he will employ the political means
whenever he can—exclusively, if possible; otherwise, in association with the economic means.
He will, at the present time, that is, have re-

Massachusetts Company, Dutch West India Company,
the Calverts, etc.—followed the traditional method of
importing exploitable human material, under bond,
from England and Europe, and also established the
chattel-slave economy by importations from Africa.
The best exposition of this phase of our history is in
Beard's *Rise of American Civilization*, vol. I, pp. 103-
109. At a later period, enormous masses of exploitable material imported themselves by immigration;
Valentine's Manual for 1859 says that in the period
1847-1858, 2,486,463 immigrants passed through the
port of New York. This competition tended to de-
press the slave-economy in the industrial sections of
the country, and to supplant it with a wage-economy.
It is noteworthy that public sentiment in those regions
did not regard the slave-economy as objectionable
until it could no longer be profitably maintained.

course to the State's modern apparatus of exploitation; the apparatus of tariffs, concessions, rent-monopoly, and the like. It is a matter of the commonest observation that this is his first instinct. So long, therefore, as the organization of the political means is available—so long as the highly-centralized bureaucratic State stands as primarily a distributor of economic advantage, an arbiter of exploitation, so long will that instinct effectively declare itself. A proletarian State would merely, like the merchant-State, shift the incidence of exploitation, and there is no historic ground for the presumption that a collectivist State would be in any essential respect unlike its predecessors; [19] as we are beginning to see, "the Russian experiment" has amounted to the erection of a highly-centralized bureaucratic State upon the ruins of another, leaving the entire apparatus of exploitation intact and ready for use. Hence, in view of the law of fundamental economics just cited, the

[19] Supposing, for example, that Mr. Norman Thomas and a solid collectivist Congress, with a solid collectivist Supreme Court, should presently fall heir to our enormously powerful apparatus of exploitation, it needs no great stretch of imagination to forecast the upshot.

expectation that collectivism will appreciably alter the essential character of the State appears illusory.

Thus the findings arrived at by the historical method amply support the immense body of practical considerations brought forward by Spencer against the State's inroads upon social power. When Spencer concludes that "in State-organizations, corruption is unavoidable," the historical method abundantly shows cause why, in the nature of things, this should be expected—*vilescit origine tali*. When Freud comments on the shocking disparity between State-ethics and private ethics—and his observations on this point are most profound and searching—the historical method at once supplies the best of reasons why that disparity should be looked for.[20] When Ortega y Gasset says that "Statism is the higher form taken by

[20] In April, 1933, the American State issued half a billion dollars' worth of bonds of small denominations, to attract investment by poor persons. It promised to pay these, principal and interest, in gold of the then-existing value. Within three months the State repudiated that promise. Such an action by an individual would, as Freud says, dishonour him forever, and mark him as no better than a knave. Done by an association of individuals, it would put them in the category of a professional-criminal class.

violence and direct action, when these are set up as standards," the historical method enables us to perceive at once that his definition is precisely that which one would make *a priori*.

The historical method, moreover, establishes the important fact that, as in the case of tabetic or parasitic diseases, the depletion of social power by the State can not be checked after a certain point of progress is passed. History does not show an instance where, once beyond this point, this depletion has not ended in complete and permanent collapse. In some cases, disintegration is slow and painful. Death set its mark on Rome at the end of the second century, but she dragged out a pitiable existence for some time after the Antonines. Athens, on the other hand, collapsed quickly. Some authorities think that Europe is dangerously near that point, if not already past it; but contemporary conjecture is probably without much value. That point may have been reached in America, and it may not; again, certainty is unattainable—plausible arguments may be made either way. Of two things, however, we may be certain: the first is, that the rate of America's approach to that point is being prodigiously accelerated; and the second is, that there is no evidence of any disposition to retard it, or any intelligent apprehension of the danger which that acceleration betokens.

3

IN CONSIDERING the State's development in America, it is important to keep in mind the fact that America's experience of the State was longer during the colonial period than during the period of American independence; the period 1607-1776 was longer than the period 1776-1935. Moreover, the colonists came here full-grown, and had already a considerable experience of the State in England and Europe before they arrived; and for purposes of comparison, this would extend the former period by a few years, say at least fifteen. It would probably be safe to put it that the American colonists had twenty-five years' longer experience of the State than citizens of the United States have had.

Their experience, too, was not only longer, but more varied. The British State, the French, Dutch, Swedish and Spanish States, were all established here. The separatist Eng-

lish dissenters who landed at Plymouth had
lived under the Dutch State as well as under
the British State. When James I made England too uncomfortable for them to live in,
they went to Holland; and many of the institutions which they subsequently set up in
New England, and which were later incorpo-
rated into the general body of what we call
"American institutions," were actually Dutch,
though commonly—almost invariably—we ac-
credit them to England. They were for the
most part Roman-Continental in their origin,
but they were transmitted here from Holland,
not from England.[1]   No such institutions
existed in England at that time, and hence
the Plymouth colonists could not have seen
them there; they could have seen them only
in Holland, where they did exist.

Our colonial period coincided with the period of revolution and readjustment in England, referred to in the preceding chapter,

[1] Among these institutions are: our system of free
public education; local self-government as originally
established in the township system; our method of
conveying land; almost all of our system of equity;
much of our criminal code; and our method of ad-
ministering estates.

when the British merchant-State was displacing the feudal State, consolidating its own position, and shifting the incidence of economic exploitation. These revolutionary measures gave rise to an extensive review of the general theory on which the feudal State had been operating. The earlier Stuarts governed on the theory of monarchy by divine right. The State's economic beneficiaries were answerable only to the monarch, who was theoretically answerable only to God; he had no responsibilities to society at large, save such as he chose to incur, and these only for the duration of his pleasure. In 1607, the year of the Virginia colony's landing at Jamestown, John Cowell, regius professor of civil law at the University of Cambridge, laid down the doctrine that the monarch "is above the law by his absolute power, and though for the better and equal course in making laws he do admit the Three Estates unto Council, yet this in divers learned men's opinions is not of constraint, but of his own benignity, or by reason of the promise made upon oath at the time of his coronation."

This doctrine, which was elaborated to the

utmost in the extraordinary work called *Patriarcha*, by Sir Robert Filmer, was all well enough so long as the line of society's stratification was clear, straight and easily drawn. The feudal State's economic beneficiaries were virtually a close corporation, a compact body consisting of a Church hierarchy and a titled group of hereditary, large-holding landed proprietors. In respect of interests, this body was extremely homogeneous, and their interests, few in number, were simple in character and easily defined. With the monarch, the hierarchy, and a small, closely-limited nobility above the line of stratification, and an undifferentiated populace below it, this theory of sovereignty was passable; it answered the purposes of the feudal State as well as any.

But the practical outcome of this theory did not, and could not, suit the purposes of the rapidly-growing class of merchants and financiers. They wished to introduce a new economic system. Under feudalism, production had been, as a general thing, for use, with the incidence of exploitation falling largely on a peasantry. The State had by no means always kept its hands off trade, but it had never countenanced the idea that its chief reason for existence was, as we say, "to help business." The merchants and financiers, however, had precisely this idea in mind. They saw the attractive possibilities of production for profit, with the incidence of exploitation gradually shifting to an industrial proletariat. They saw also, however, that to realize all these possibilities, they must get the State's mechanism to working as smoothly and powerfully on the side of "business" as it had been working on the side of the monarchy, the Church, and the large-holding landed proprietors. This meant capturing control of this mechanism, and so altering and adapting it as to give themselves the same free access to the political means as was enjoyed by the displaced beneficiaries. The course by which they accomplished this is marked by the Civil War, the dethronement and execution of Charles I, the Puritan protectorate, and the revolution of 1688.

This is the actual inwardness of what is known as the Puritan movement in England. It had a quasi-religious motivation—speaking strictly, an ecclesiological motivation—but the paramount practical end towards which it tended was a repartition of access to the political means. It is a significant fact, though seldom noticed, that the only tenet with which Puritanism managed to evangelize equally the non-Christian and Christian world of English-bred civilization is its tenet of work, its doctrine that work is, by God's express will and command, a duty; indeed almost, if not quite, the first and most important of man's secular duties. This erection of labour into a Christian virtue *per se,* this investment of work with a special religious sanction, was an invention of Puritanism; it was something never heard of in England before the rise of the Puritan State. The only doctrine antedating it presented labour as the means to a purely secular end; as Cranmer's divines put it, "that I may learn and labour truly to get mine own living." There is no hint that God would take it amiss if one preferred to do little work and put up with a poor living, for the sake of doing something else with one's time. Perhaps the best witness to the essential character of the Puritan movement in England and America is the thoroughness with which its doctrine of work has pervaded both literatures, all the way from Cromwell's letters to Carlyle's panegyric and Longfellow's verse.

But the merchant-State of the Puritans was like any other; it followed the standard pattern. It originated in conquest and confiscation, like the feudal State which it displaced; the only difference being that its conquest was by civil war instead of foreign war. Its object was the economic exploitation of one class by another; for the exploitation of feudal serfs by a nobility, it proposed only to substitute the exploitation of a proletariat by enterprisers. Like its predecessor, the merchant-State was purely an organization of the political means, a machine for the distribution of economic advantage, but with its mechanism adapted to the requirements of a more numerous and more highly differentiated order of beneficiaries; a class, moreover, whose numbers were not limited by heredity or by the sheer arbitrary pleasure of a monarch.

The process of establishing the merchant-State, however, necessarily brought about changes in the general theory of sovereignty. The bald doctrine of Cowell and Filmer was

no longer practicable; yet any new theory had
to find room for some sort of divine sanction,
for the habit of men's minds does not change
suddenly, and Puritanism's alliance between
religious and secular interests was extremely
close.   One may not quite put it that the
merchant-enterprisers made use of religious
fanaticism to pull their chestnuts out of the
fire; the religionists had sound and good chestnuts of their own to look after.   They had
plenty of rabid nonsense to answer for, plenty
of sour hypocrisy, plenty of vicious fanaticism;
whenever we think of seventeenth-century
British Puritanism, we think of Hugh Peters,
of Praise-God Barebones, of Cromwell's icono-
clasts "smashing the mighty big angels in
glass."   But behind all this untowardness there
was in the religionists a body of sound conscience, soundly and justly outraged; and no
doubt, though mixed with an intolerable deal
of unscrupulous greed, there was on the part
of the merchant-enterprisers a sincere persuasion that what was good for business was good
for society.   Taking Hampden's conscience as
representative, one would say that it operated

under the limitations set by nature upon the typical sturdy Buckinghamshire squire; the mercantile conscience was likewise ill-informed, and likewise set its course with a hard, dogged, provincial stubbornness. Still, the alliance of the two bodies of conscience was not without some measure of respectability. No doubt, for example, Hampden regarded the State-controlled episcopate to some extent objectively, as unscriptural in theory, and a tool of Antichrist in practice; and no doubt, too, the mercantile conscience, with the disturbing vision of William Laud in view, might have found State-managed episcopacy objectionable on other grounds than those of special interest.

The merchant-State's political rationale had to respond to the pressure of a growing individualism. The spirit of individualism appeared in the latter half of the sixteenth century; probably—as well as such obscure origins can be determined—as a by-product of the Continental revival of learning, or, it may be, specifically as a by-product of the Reformation in Germany. It was long, however, in gaining force enough to make itself count in shaping political theory. The feudal State could take no account of this spirit; its stark régime of status was operable only where there was no great multiplicity of diverse economic interests to be accommodated, and where the sum of social power remained practically stable. Under the British feudal State, one large-holding landed proprietor's interest was much like another's, and one bishop's or clergyman's interest was about the same in kind as another's. The interests of the monarchy and court were not greatly diversified, and the sum of social power varied but little from time to time. Hence an economic class-solidarity was easily maintained; access upward from one class to the other was easily blocked, so easily that very few positive State-interventions were necessary to keep people, as we say, in their place; or as Cranmer's divines put it, to keep them doing their duty in that station of life unto which it had pleased God to call them. Thus the State could accomplish its primary purpose, and still afford to remain relatively weak. It could normally, that is, enable a thorough-going economic exploitation with relatively little apparatus of legislation or of personnel.[2]

The merchant-State, on the other hand, with its ensuing régime of contract, had to meet the problem set by a rapid development of social power, and a multiplicity of economic interests. Both these tended to foster and stimulate the spirit of individualism. The management of social power made the merchant-enterpriser feel that he was quite as much somebody as anybody, and that the general order of interest which he represented—and in particular his own special fraction of that interest—was to be regarded as most respectable, which hitherto it had not been. In short, he had a full sense of himself as an individual, which on these grounds he could of course justify beyond peradventure. The aristocratic disparagement of his pursuits, and the conse-

[2] Throughout Europe, indeed, up to the close of the eighteenth century, the State was quite weak, even considering the relatively moderate development of social power, and the moderate amount of economic accumulation available to its predatory purposes. Social power in modern France could pay the flat annual levy of Louis XIV's taxes without feeling it, and would like nothing better than to commute the republican State's levy on those terms.

quent stigma of inferiority which had been so long fixed upon the "base mechanical," exacerbated this sense, and rendered it at its best assertive, and at its worst, disposed to exaggerate the characteristic defects of his class as well as its excellences, and lump them off together in a new category of social virtues—its hardness, ruthlessness, ignorance and vulgarity at par with its commercial integrity, its shrewdness, diligence and thrift. Thus the fully-developed composite type of merchant-enterpriser-financier might be said to run all the psychological gradations between the brothers Cheeryble at one end of the scale, and Mr. Gradgrind, Sir Gorgius Midas and Mr. Bottles at the other.

This individualism fostered the formulation of certain doctrines which in one shape or another found their way into the official political philosophy of the merchant-State. Foremost among these were the two which the Declaration of Independence lays down as fundamental, the doctrine of natural rights and the doctrine of popular sovereignty. In a generation which had exchanged the authority of a pope for the authority of a book—or rather, the authority of unlimited private interpretation of a book—there was no difficulty about finding ample Scriptural sanction for both these doctrines. The interpretation of the Bible, like the judicial interpretation of a constitution, is merely a process by which, as a contemporary of Bishop Butler said, anything may be made to mean anything; and in the absence of a coercive authority, papal, conciliar or judicial, any given interpretation finds only such acceptance as may, for whatever reason, be accorded it. Thus the episode of Eden, the parable of the talents, the Apostolic injunction against being "slothful in business," were a warrant for the Puritan doctrine of work; they brought the sanction of Scripture and the sanction of economic interest into complete agreement, uniting the religionist and the merchant-enterpriser in the bond of a common intention. Thus, again, the view of man as made in the image of God, made only a little lower than the angels, the subject of so august a transaction as the Atonement, quite corroborated the political doctrine of his endowment by his Creator with certain rights unalienable by Church or State. While the merchant-enterpriser might hold with Mr. Jefferson that the truth of this political doctrine is self-evident, its Scriptural support was yet of great value as carrying an implication of human nature's dignity which braced his more or less diffident and self-conscious individualism; and the doctrine that so dignified him might easily be conceived of as dignifying his pursuits. Indeed, the Bible's indorsement of the doctrine of labour and the doctrine of natural rights was really his charter for rehabilitating "trade" against the disparagement that the régime of status had put upon it, and for investing it with the most brilliant lustre of respectability.

In the same way, the doctrine of popular sovereignty could be mounted on impregnable Scriptural ground. Civil society was an association of true believers functioning for common secular purposes; and its right of self-government with respect to these purposes was God-given. If on the religious side all believers were priests, then on the secular side they were all sovereigns; the notion of an intervening *jure divino* monarch was as repugnant to Scripture as that of an intervening *jure divino* pope—witness the Israelite commonwealth upon which monarchy was visited as explicitly a punishment for sin. Civil legislation was supposed to interpret and particularize the laws of God as revealed in the Bible, and its administrators were responsible to the congregation in both its religious and secular capacities. Where the revealed law was silent, legislation · was to be guided by its general spirit, as best this might be determined. These principles obviously left open a considerable area of choice; but hypothetically the range of civil liberty and the range of religious liberty had a common boundary.

This religious sanction of popular sovereignty was agreeable to the merchant-enterpriser; it fell in well with his individualism, enhancing considerably his sense of personal dignity and consequence. He could regard himself as by birthright not only a free citizen of a heavenly commonwealth, but also a free elector in an earthly commonwealth fashioned, as nearly as might be, after the heavenly pattern. The range of liberty permitted him in both qualities was satisfactory; he could summon warrant of Scripture to cover his under-

takings both here and hereafter. As far as
this present world's concerns went, his doctrine of labour was Scriptural, his doctrine of
master-and-servant was Scriptural—even bond-
service, even chattel-service was Scriptural; his
doctrine of a wage-economy, of money-lending
—again the parable of the talents—both were
Scriptural. What especially recommended the
doctrine of popular sovereignty to him on its
secular side, however, was the immense lev-
erage it gave for ousting the régime of status
to make way for the régime of contract; in a
word, for displacing the feudal State and bringing in the merchant-State.

But interesting as these two doctrines were,
their actual application was a matter of great
difficulty. On the religious side, the doctrine
of natural rights had to take account of the
unorthodox. Theoretically it was easy to dispose of them. The separatists, for example,
such as those who manned the *Mayflower,* had
lost their natural rights in the fall of Adam,
and had never made use of the means appointed to reclaim them. This was all very
well, but the logical extension of this principle into actual practice was a rather grave

affair. There were a good many dissenters, all told, and they were articulate on the matter of natural rights, which made trouble; so that when all was said and done, the doctrine came out considerably compromised. Then, in respect of popular sovereignty, there were the Presbyterians. Calvinism was monocratic to the core; in fact, Presbyterianism existed side by side with episcopacy in the Church of England in the sixteenth century, and was nudged out only very gradually.[3] They were a numerous body, and in point of Scripture and history they had a great deal to say for their position. Thus the practical task of organizing a spiritual commonwealth had as hard going with the logic of popular sovereignty as it had with the logic of natural rights.

[3] During the reign of Elizabeth the Puritan contention, led by Cartwright, was for what amounted to a theory of *jure divino* Presbyterianism. The Establishment at large took the position of Archbishop Whitgift and Richard Hooker that the details of church polity were indifferent, and therefore properly subject to State regulation. The High Church doctrine of *jure divino* episcopacy was laid down later, by Whitgift's successor, Bancroft. Thus up to 1604 the Presbyterians were objectionable on secular grounds, and afterwards on both secular and ecclesiastical grounds.

The task of secular organization was even more troublesome. A society organized in conformity to these two principles is easily conceivable—such an organization as Paine and the Declaration contemplated, for example, arising out of social agreement, and concerning itself only with the maintenance of freedom and security for the individual—but the practical task of effecting such an organization is quite another matter. On general grounds, doubtless, the Puritans would have found this impracticable; if, indeed, the times are ever to be ripe for anything of the kind, their times were certainly not. The particular ground of difficulty, however, was that the merchant-enterpriser did not want that form of social organization; in fact, one can not be sure that the Puritan religionists themselves wanted it. The root-trouble was, in short, that there was no practicable way to avert a shattering collision between the logic of natural rights and popular sovereignty, and the economic law that man tends always to satisfy his needs and desires with the least possible exertion.

This law governed the merchant-enterpriser in common with the rest of mankind. He was not for an organization that should do no more than maintain freedom and security; he was for one that should redistribute access to the political means, and concern itself with freedom and security only so far as would be consistent with keeping this access open. That is to say, he was thoroughly indisposed to the idea of *government;* he was quite as strong for the idea of *the State* as the hierarchy and nobility were. He was not for any essential transformation in the State's character, but merely for a repartition of the economic advantages that the State confers.

Thus the merchant-polity amounted to an attempt, more or less disingenuous, at reconciling matters which in their nature can not be reconciled. The ideas of natural rights and popular sovereignty were, as we have seen, highly acceptable and highly animating to all the forces allied against the feudal idea; but while these ideas might be easily reconcilable with a system of simple government, such a system would not answer the purpose. Only the State-system would do that. The problem therefore was, how to keep these ideas well in the forefront of political theory, and at the same time prevent their practical application from undermining the organization of the political means. It was a difficult problem. The best that could be done with it was by making certain structural alterations in the State, which would give it the appearance of expressing these ideas, without the reality. The most important of these structural changes was that of bringing in the so-called representative or parliamentary system, which Puritanism introduced into the modern world, and which has received a great deal of praise as an advance towards democracy. This praise, however, is exaggerated. The change was one of form only, and its bearing on democracy has been inconsiderable.[4]

II

The migration of Englishmen to America merely transferred this problem into another setting. The discussion of political theory

[4] So were the kaleidoscopic changes that took place in France after the revolution of 1789. Throughout the Directorate, the Consulship, the Restoration, the two Empires, the three Republics and the Commune, the French State kept its essential character intact; it remained always the organization of the political means.

went on vigorously, but the philosophy of natural rights and popular sovereignty came out in practice about where they had come out in England. Here again a great deal has been made of the democratic spirit and temper of the migrants, especially in the case of the separatists who landed at Plymouth, but the facts do not bear it out, except with regard to the decentralizing congregationalist principle of church order. This principle of lodging final authority in the smallest unit rather than the largest—in the local congregation rather than in a synod or general council—was democratic, and its thorough-going application in a scheme of church order would represent some actual advance towards democracy, and give some recognition to the general philosophy of natural rights and popular sovereignty. The Plymouth settlers did something with this principle, actually applying it in the matter of church order, and for this they deserve credit.[5] Applying it in the matter of civil

[5] In 1629 the Massachusetts Bay colony adopted the Plymouth colony's model of congregational autonomy, but finding its principle dangerously inconsistent with the principle of the State, almost immediately nullified their action; retaining, however, the name of

order, however, was another affair. It is true
that the Plymouth colonists probably contemplated something of the kind, and that for a
time they practised a sort of primitive communism. They drew up an agreement on
shipboard which may be taken at its face value
as evidence of their democratic disposition,
though it was not in any sense a "frame of
government," like Penn's, or any kind of constitutional document. Those who speak of it
as our first written constitution are considerably in advance of their text, for it was merely
an agreement to make a constitution or "frame
of government" when the settlers should have
come to land and looked the situation over.
One sees that it could hardly have been more
than this—indeed, that the proposed constitution itself could be no more than provisional—
when it is remembered that these migrants

Congregationalism. This mode of masquerade is
easily recognizable as one of the modern State's most
useful expedients for maintaining the appearance of
things without the reality. The names of our two
largest political parties will at once appear as a capital example. Within two years the Bay colony had
set up a State church, nominally congregationalist,
but actually a branch of the civil service, as in England.

were not their own men. They did not sail
on their own, nor were they headed for any
unpreëmpted territory on which they might
establish a squatter sovereignty and set up any
kind of civil order they saw fit. They were
headed for Virginia, to settle in the jurisdiction of a company of English merchant-enterprisers, now growing shaky, and soon to be
superseded by the royal authority, and its territory converted into a royal province. It was
only by misreckonings and the accidents of navigation that, most unfortunately for the prospects of the colony, the settlers landed on the
stern and rockbound coast of Plymouth.

These settlers were in most respects probably as good as the best who ever found their
way to America. They were bred of what
passed in England as "the lower orders," sober,
hard-working and capable, and their residence
under Continental institutions in Holland had
given them a fund of politico-religious ideas
and habits of thought which set them considerably apart from the rest of their countrymen. There is, however, no more than an
antiquarian interest in determining how far
they were actually possessed by those ideas.

They may have contemplated a system of complete religious and civil democracy, or they may not. They may have found their communist practices agreeable to their notion of a sound and just social order, or they may not. The point is that while apparently they might be free enough to found a church order as democratic as they chose, they were by no means free to found a civil democracy, or anything remotely resembling one, because they were in bondage to the will of an English trading-company. Even their religious freedom was permissive; the London company simply cared nothing about that. The same considerations governed their communistic practices; whether or not these practices suited their ideas, they were obliged to adopt them. Their agreement with the London merchant-enterprisers bound them, in return for transportation and outfit, to seven years' service, during which time they should work on a system of common-land tillage, store their produce in a common warehouse, and draw their maintenance from these common stores. Thus whether or not they were communists in principle, their actual practice of communism was by prescription.

The fundamental fact to be observed in any survey of the American State's initial development is the one whose importance was first remarked, I believe, by Mr. Beard; that the trading-company—the commercial corporation for colonization—was actually an autonomous State. "Like the State," says Mr. Beard, "it had a constitution, a charter issued by the Crown . . . like the State, it had a territorial basis, a grant of land often greater in area than a score of European principalities . . . it could make assessments, coin money, regulate trade, dispose of corporate property, collect taxes, manage a treasury, and provide for defense. Thus"—and here is the important observation, so important that I venture to italicize it—"*every essential element long afterward found in the government of the American State appeared in the chartered corporation that started English civilization in America.*" Generally speaking, the system of civil order established in America was the State-system of the "mother countries" operating over a considerable body of water; the only thing that distinguished it was that the exploited and dependent class was situated at an unusual distance from the owning and exploiting class. The headquarters of the autonomous State were on one side of the Atlantic, and its subjects on the other.

This separation gave rise to administrative difficulties of one kind and another; and to obviate them—perhaps for other reasons as well—one English company, the Massachusetts Bay Company, moved over bodily in 1630, bringing their charter and most of their stockholders with them, thus setting up an actual autonomous State in America. The thing to be observed about this is that the merchant-State was set up complete in New England long before it was set up in Old England. Most of the English immigrants to Massachusetts came over between 1630 and 1640; and in this period the English merchant-State was only at the beginning of its hardest struggles for supremacy. James I died in 1625, and his successor, Charles I, continued his absolutist régime. From 1629, the year in which the Bay Company was chartered, to 1640, when the Long Parliament was called, he

ruled without a parliament, effectively sup-
pressing what few vestiges of liberty had survived the Tudor and Jacobean tyrannies; and
during these eleven years the prospects of the
English merchant-State were at their lowest.[6]
It still had to face the distractions of the Civil
War, the retarding anomalies of the Commonwealth, the Restoration, and the recurrence of
tyrannical absolutism under James II, before it
succeeded in establishing itself firmly through
the revolution of 1688.

On the other hand, the leaders of the Bay
Colony were free from the first to establish a
State-policy of their own devising, and to set
up a State-structure which should express that
policy without compromise. There was no
competing policy to extinguish, no rival structure to refashion. Thus the merchant-State
came into being in a clear field a full half-
century before it attained supremacy in England. Competition of any kind, or the possibility of competition, it has never had. A

[6] Probably it was a forecast of this state of things,
as much as the greater convenience of administration,
that caused the Bay Company to move over to Massachusetts, bag and baggage, in the year following the
issuance of their charter.

point of greatest importance to remember is
that the merchant-State is the only form of the
State that ever existed in America. Whether
under the rule of a trading-company or a
provincial governor or a republican representative legislature, Americans have never
known any other form of the State. In this
respect the Massachusetts Bay colony is differentiated only as being the first autonomous
State ever established in America, and as fur-
nishing the most complete and convenient
example for purposes of study. In principle
it was not differentiated. The State in New
England, Virginia, Maryland, the Jerseys, New
York, Connecticut, everywhere, was purely a
class-State, with control of the political means
reposing in the hands of what we now style, in
a general way, the "business-man."

In the eleven years of Charles's tyrannical
absolutism, English immigrants came over to
join the Bay colony, at the rate of about two
thousand a year. No doubt at the outset some
of the colonists had the idea of becoming agricultural specialists, as in Virginia, and of maintaining certain vestiges, or rather imitations,
of semi-feudal social practice, such as were

possible under that form of industry when operated by a slave-economy or a tenant-economy. This, however, proved impracticable; the climate and soil of New England were against it. A tenant-economy was precarious, for rather than work for a master, the immigrant agriculturist naturally preferred to push out into unpreëmpted land, and work for himself; in other words, as Turgôt, Marx, Hertzka, and many others have shown, he could not be exploited until he had been expropriated from the land. The long and hard winters took the profit out of slave-labour in agriculture. The Bay colonists experimented with it, however, even attempting to enslave the Indians, which they found could not be done, for the reasons that I have already noticed. In default of this, the colonists carried out the primitive technique by resorting to extermination, their ruthless ferocity being equalled only by that of the Virginia colonists.[7] They held some

[7] Thomas Robinson Hazard, the Rhode Island Quaker, in his delightful *Jonnycake Papers*, says that the Great Swamp Fight of 1675 was "instigated against the rightful owners of the soil, solely by the cussed godly Puritans of Massachusetts, and their hell-hound allies, the Presbyterians of Connecticut; whom, though charity is my specialty, I can never

slaves, and did a great deal of slave-trading; but in the main, they became at the outset a race of small freeholding farmers, shipbuilders, navigators, maritime enterprisers in fish, whales, molasses, rum, and miscellaneous cargoes; and presently, moneylenders. Their remarkable success in these pursuits is well known; it is worth mention here in order to account for many of the complications and collisions of interest subsequently ensuing upon the merchant-State's fundamental doctrine that the primary function of government is not to maintain freedom and security, but to "help business."

III

One examines the American merchant-State in vain for any suggestion of the philosophy of natural rights and popular sovereignty. The company-system and the provincial sys-

think of without feeling as all good Rhode Islanders should, . . . and as old Miss Hazard did when in like vein she thanked God in the Conanicut prayer-meeting that she could hold malice forty years." The Rhode Island settlers dealt with the Indians for rights in land, and made friends with them.

tem made no place for it, and the one autonomous State was uncompromisingly against it.
The Bay Company brought over their charter
to serve as the constitution of the new colony,
and under its provisions the form of the State
was that of an uncommonly small and close
oligarchy. The right to vote was vested only
in shareholding members, or "freemen" of
the corporation, on the stark State principle
laid down many years later by John Jay, that
"those who own the country should govern the
country." At the end of a year, the Bay colony
comprised perhaps about two thousand persons; and of these, certainly not twenty, probably not more than a dozen, had anything
whatever to say about its government. This
small group constituted itself as a sort of directorate or council, appointing its own executive. body, which consisted of a governor, a
lieutenant-governor, and a half-dozen or more
magistrates. These officials had no responsibility to the community at large, but only to
the directorate. By the terms of the charter,
the directorate was self-perpetuating. It was
permitted to fill vacancies and add to its numbers as it saw fit; and in so doing it followed a

policy similar to that which was subsequently recommended by Alexander Hamilton, of admitting only such well-to-do and influential persons as could be trusted to sustain a solid front against anything savouring of popular sovereignty.

Historians have very properly made a great deal of the influence of Calvinist theology in bracing the strongly anti-democratic attitude of the Bay Company. The story is readable and interesting—often amusing—yet the gist of it is so simple that it can be perceived at once. The company's principle of action was in this respect the one that in like circumstances has for a dozen centuries invariably motivated the State. The Marxian dictum that "religion is the opiate of the people" is either an ignorant or a slovenly confusion of terms, which can not be too strongly reprehended. Religion was never that, nor will it ever be; but organized Christianity, which is by no means the same thing as religion, has been the opiate of the people ever since the beginning of the fourth century, and never has this opiate been employed for political purposes more skilfully than it was by the Massachusetts Bay oligarchy.

In the year 311 the Roman emperor Constantine issued an edict of toleration in favour of organized Christianity. He patronized the new cult heavily, giving it rich presents, and even adopted the labarum as his standard, which was a most distinguished gesture, and cost nothing; the story of the heavenly sign appearing before his crucial battle against Maxentius may quite safely be put down beside that of the apparitions seen before the battle of the Marne. He never joined the Church, however, and the tradition that he was converted to Christianity is open to great doubt. The point of all this is that circumstances had by that time made Christianity a considerable figure; it had survived contumely and persecution, and had become a social influence which Constantine saw was destined to reach far enough to make it worth courting. The Church could be made a most effective tool of the State, and only a very moderate amount of statesmanship was needed to discern the right way of bringing this about. The understanding, undoubtedly tacit, was based on a simple *quid pro quo;* in exchange for imperial recognition and patronage, and

endowments enough to keep up to the requirements of a high official respectability, the
Church should quit its disagreeable habit of
criticizing the course of politics; and in particular, it should abstain from unfavourable
comment on the State's administration of the
political means.

These are the unvarying terms—again I say,
undoubtedly tacit, as it is seldom necessary to
stipulate against biting the hand by which one
is fed—of every understanding that has been
struck since Constantine's day, between organized Christianity and the State. They were
the terms of the understanding struck in the
Germanies and in England at the Reformation. The petty German principality had its
State Church as it had its State theatre; and
in England, Henry VIII set up the Church in
its present status as an arm of the civil service,
like the Post-office. The fundamental understanding in all cases was that the Church should
not interfere with or disparage the organization of the political means; and in practice it
naturally followed that the Church would go
further, and quite regularly abet this organization to the best of its ability.

The merchant-State in America came to this understanding with organized Christianity. In the Bay colony the Church became in 1638 an established subsidiary of the State,[8] supported by taxation; it maintained a State creed, promulgated in 1647. In some other colonies also, as for example, in Virginia, the Church was a branch of the State service, and where it was not actually established as such, the same understanding was reached by other means, quite as satisfactory. Indeed, the merchant-State both in England and America soon became lukewarm towards the idea of an Establishment, perceiving that the same *modus vivendi* could be almost as easily arrived at under voluntaryism, and that the latter had the advantage of satisfying practically all modes of credal and ceremonial preference,

[8] Mr. Parrington (*Main Currents in American Thought*, vol. I, p. 24) cites the successive steps leading up to this, as follows: the law of 1631, restricting the franchise to Church members; of 1635, obliging all persons to attend Church services; and of 1636, which established a virtual State monopoly, by requiring consent of both Church and State authority before a new church could be set up. Roger Williams observed acutely that a State establishment of organized Christianity is "a politic invention of man to maintain the civil State."

thus releasing the State from the troublesome
and profitless business of interference in dis-
putes over matters of doctrine and Church
order.

Voluntaryism pure and simple was set up
in Rhode Island by Roger Williams, John
Clarke, and their associates who were banished
from the Bay colony almost exactly three hundred years ago, in 1636. This group of exiles
is commonly regarded as having founded a
society on the philosophy of natural rights and
popular sovereignty in respect of both Church
order and civil order, and as having launched
an experiment in democracy. This, however,
is an exaggeration. The leaders of the group
were undoubtedly in sight of this philosophy,
and as far as Church order is concerned, their
practice was conformable to it. On the civil
side, the most that can be said is that their
practice was conformable in so far as they knew
how to make it so; and one says this much
only by a very considerable concession. The
least that can be said, on the other hand, is
that their practice was for a time greatly in
advance of the practice prevailing in other
colonies—so far in advance that Rhode Island

was in great disrepute with its neighbours in Massachusetts and Connecticut, who diligently disseminated the tale of its evil fame throughout the land, with the customary exaggerations and embellishments.   Nevertheless, through acceptance of the State system of land-tenure, the political structure of Rhode Island was a State-structure from the outset, contemplating as it did the stratification of society into an owning and exploiting class and a propertyless dependent class.   Williams's theory of the State was that of social compact arrived at among equals, but equality did not exist in Rhode Island; the actual outcome was a pure class-State.

In the spring of 1638, Williams acquired about twenty square miles of land by gift from two Indian sachems, in addition to some he had bought from them two years before.   In October he formed a "proprietary" of purchasers who bought twelve-thirteenths of the Indian grant.   Bicknell, in his history of Rhode Island, cites a letter written by Williams to the deputy-governor of the Bay colony, which says frankly that the plan of this proprietary contemplated the creation of two classes of citizens, one consisting of landholding heads of families, and the other, of "young men, single persons" who were a landless tenantry, and as Bicknell says, "had no voice or vote as to the officers of the community, or the laws which they were called upon to obey." Thus the civil order in Rhode Island was essentially a pure State order, as much so as the civil order of the Bay colony, or any other in America; and in fact the landed-property franchise lasted uncommonly long in Rhode Island, existing there for some time after it had been given up in most other quarters of America.[9]

By way of summing up, it is enough to say that nowhere in the American colonial civil

[9] Bicknell says that the formation of Williams's proprietary was "a landholding, land-jobbing, land-selling scheme, with no moral, social, civil, educational or religious end in view"; and his discussion of the early land-allotments on the site where the city of Providence now stands, makes it pretty clear that "the first years of Providence are consumed in a greedy scramble for land." Bicknell is not precisely an unfriendly witness towards Williams, though his history is avowedly *ex parte* for the thesis that the true expounder of civil freedom in Rhode Island was not Williams, but Clarke. This contention is immaterial to the present purpose, however, for the State system of land-tenure prevailed in Clarke's settlements on Aquidneck as it did in Williams's settlements farther up the bay.

order was there ever the trace of a democracy. The political structure was always that of the merchant-State; Americans have never known any other. Furthermore, the philosophy of natural rights and popular sovereignty was never once exhibited anywhere in American political practice during the colonial period, from the first settlement in 1607 down to the revolution of 1776.

4

AFTER conquest and confiscation have been effected, and the State set up, its first concern is with the land. The State assumes the right of eminent domain over its territorial basis, whereby every landholder becomes in theory a tenant of the State. In its capacity as ultimate landlord, the State distributes the land among its beneficiaries on its own terms. A point to be observed in passing is that by the State-system of land-tenure each original transaction confers two distinct monopolies, entirely different in their nature, inasmuch as one concerns the right to labour-made property, and the other concerns the right to purely law-made property. The one is a monopoly of the use-value of land; and the other, a monopoly of the economic rent of land. The first gives the right to keep other persons from using the land in question, or trespassing on it, and the right to exclusive possession of values

accruing from the application of labour to it;
values, that is, which are produced by exercise
of the economic means upon the particular
property in question. Monopoly of economic
rent, on the other hand, gives the exclusive
right to values accruing from the desire of
other persons to possess that property; values
which take their rise irrespective of any exercise of the economic means on the part of the
holder.[1]

Economic rent arises when, for whatsoever
reason, two or more persons compete for the
possession of a piece of land, and it increases
directly according to the number of persons
competing. The whole of Manhattan Island
was bought originally by a handful of Hol-
landers from a handful of Indians for twenty-

[1] The economic rent of the Trinity Church estate
in New York City, for instance, would be as high as
it is now, even if the holders had never done a stroke
of work on the property. Landowners who are holding a property "for a rise" usually leave it idle, or
improve it only to the extent necessary to clear its
taxes; the type of building commonly called a "tax-
payer" is a familiar sight everywhere. Twenty-five
years ago a member of the New York City Tax Commission told me that by careful estimate there was
almost enough vacant land within the city limits to
feed the population, assuming that all of it were
arable and put under intensive cultivation!

four dollars' worth of trinkets. The subsequent "rise in land-values," as we call it, was brought about by the steady influx of population and the consequent high competition for portions of the island's surface; and these ensuing values were monopolized by the holders. They grew to an enormous size, and the holders profited accordingly; the Astor, Wendel, and Trinity Church estates have always served as classical examples for study of the State-system of land-tenure.

Bearing in mind that the State is the organization of the political means—that its primary intention is to enable the economic exploitation of one class by another—we see that it has always acted on the principle already cited, that expropriation must precede exploitation. There is no other way to make the political means effective. The first postulate of fundamental economics is that man is a land-animal, deriving his subsistence wholly from the land.[2] His entire wealth is produced by the applica-

[2] As a technical term in economics, *land* includes all natural resources, earth, air, water, sunshine, timber and minerals *in situ*, etc. Failure to understand this use of the term has seriously misled some writers, notably Count Tolstoy.

tion of labour and capital to land; no form of wealth known to man can be produced in any other way. Hence, if his free access to land be shut off by legal preëmption, he can apply his labour and capital only with the land-holder's consent, and on the landholder's terms; in other words, it is at this point, and this point only, that exploitation becomes practicable.[3] Therefore the first concern of the State must be invariably, as we find it invariably is, with its policy of land-tenure.

I state these elementary matters as briefly as I can; the reader may easily find a full exposition of them elsewhere.[4] I am here concerned only to show why the State system of land-tenure came into being, and why its maintenance is necessary to the State's existence. If this system were broken up, obviously the reason for the State's existence would disap-

[3] Hence there is actually no such thing as a "labour-problem," for no encroachment on the rights of either labour or capital can possibly take place until all natural resources within reach have been preëmpted. What we call the "problem of the unemployed" is in no sense a problem, but a direct consequence of State-created monopoly.

[4] For fairly obvious reasons they have no place in the conventional courses that are followed in our schools and colleges.

pear, and the State itself would disappear with it.[5] With this in mind, it is interesting to observe that although all our public policies would seem to be in process of exhaustive review, no publicist has anything to say about the State system of land-tenure. This is no doubt the best evidence of its importance.[6]

[5] The French school of physiocrats, led by Quesnay, du Pont de Nemours, Turgôt, Gournay and le Trosne —usually regarded as the founders of the science of political economy—broached the idea of destroying this system by the confiscation of economic rent; and this idea was worked out in detail some years ago in America by Henry George. None of these writers, however, seemed to be aware of the effect that their plan would produce upon the State itself. Collectivism, on the other hand, proposes immeasurably to strengthen and entrench the State by confiscation of the use-value as well as the rental-value of land, doing away with private proprietorship in either.

[6] If one were not aware of the highly explosive character of this subject, it would be almost incredible that until three years ago, no one has ever presumed to write a history of land-speculation in America. In 1932, the firm of Harpers published an excellent work by Professor Sakolski, under the frivolous catch-penny title of *The Great American Land Bubble*. I do not believe that anyone can have a competent understanding of our history or of the character of our people, without hard study of this book. It does not pretend to be more than a preliminary approach to the subject, a sort of pathbreaker for the exhaustive treatise which someone, preferably Professor Sakolski himself, should be un-

Under the feudal State there was no great amount of traffic in land. When William, for example, set up the Norman State in England after conquest and confiscation in 1066-76, his associate banditti, among whom he parcelled out the confiscated territory, did nothing to speak of in the way of developing their holdings, and did not contemplate gain from the increment of rental-values. In fact, economic rent hardly existed; their fellow-beneficiaries were not in the market to any great extent, and the dispossessed population did not represent any economic demand. The feudal régime was a régime of status, under which landed estates yielded hardly any rental-value, and only a moderate use-value, but carried an enormous insignia-value. Land was regarded more as a badge of nobility than as an active asset; its possession marked a man as belonging to the exploiting class, and the size of his holdings seems to have counted for more than the number of his exploitable dependents.[7]

dertaking; but for what it is, nothing could be better. I am making liberal use of it throughout this section.

[7] Regard for this insignia-value or token-value of land has shown an interesting persistence. The rise of the merchant-State, supplanting the régime of

The encroachments of the merchant-State, however, brought about a change in these circumstances. The importance of rental-values was recognized, and speculative trading in land became general.

Hence in a study of the merchant-State as it appeared full-blown in America, it is a point of utmost consequence to remember that from the time of the first colonial settlement to the present day, America has been regarded as a practically limitless field for speculation in rental-values.[8] One may say at a safe venture

status by the régime of contract, opened the way for men of all sorts and conditions to climb into the exploiting class; and the new recruits have usually shown a hankering for the old distinguishing sign of their having done so, even though the rise in rental-values has made the gratification of this desire progressively costly.

[8] If our geographical development had been determined in a natural way, by the demands of use instead of the demands of speculation, our western frontier would not yet be anywhere near the Mississippi River. Rhode Island is the most thickly-populated member of the Union, yet one may drive from one end of it to the other on one of its "through" highways, and see hardly a sign of human occupancy. All discussions of "over-population" from Malthus down, are based on the premise of legal occupancy instead of actual occupancy, and are therefore utterly incompetent and worthless. Oppenheimer's calculation, made in 1912, to which I have already referred, shows

that every colonial enterpriser and proprietor after Raleigh's time understood economic rent and the conditions necessary to enhance it. The Swedish, Dutch and British trading-companies understood this; Endicott and Winthrop, of the autonomous merchant-State on the Bay, understood it; so did Penn and the Calverts; so did the Carolinian proprietors, to whom Charles II granted a lordly belt of territory south of Virginia, reaching from the Atlantic to the Pacific; and as we have seen, Roger Williams and Clarke understood it perfectly. Indeed, land-speculation may be put down as the first major industry established in colonial America. Professor Sakolski calls attention to the fact that it was flourishing in the South before the commercial importance of either negroes or tobacco was recognized. These two

that if legal occupation were abolished, every family of five persons could possess nearly twenty acres of land, and still leave about two-thirds of the planet unoccupied. Henry George's examination of Malthus's theory of population is well known, or at least, easily available. It is perhaps worth mention in passing that exaggerated rental-values are responsible for the perennial troubles of the American single-crop farmer. Curiously, one finds this fact set forth in the report of a farm-survey, published by the Department of Agriculture about fifty years ago.

staples came fully into their own about 1670—
tobacco perhaps a little earlier, but not much—
and before that, England and Europe had been
well covered by a lively propaganda of South-
ern landholders, advertising for settlers.[9]

Mr. Sakolski makes it clear that very few
original enterprisers in American rental-values
ever got much profit out of their ventures.
This is worth remarking here as enforcing the
point that what gives rise to economic rent is
the presence of a population engaged in a settled exercise of the economic means, or as we
commonly put it, "working for a living"—or
again, in technical terms, applying labour and
capital to natural resources for the production
of wealth. It was no doubt a very fine dignified
thing for Carteret, Berkeley, and their associate

[9] Mr. Chinard, professor in the Faculty of Literature at Johns Hopkins, has lately published a translation of a little book, hardly more than a pamphlet,
written in 1686 by the Huguenot refugee Durand,
giving a description of Virginia for the information
of his fellow-exiles. It strikes a modern reader as
being very favourable to Virginia, and one is amused
to read that the landholders who had entertained
Durand with an eye to business, thought he had not
laid it on half thick enough, and were much disgusted.
The book is delightfully interesting, and well worth
owning.

nobility to be the owners of a province as large as the Carolinas, but if no population were settled there, producing wealth by exercise of the economic means, obviously not a foot of it would bear a pennyworth of rental-value, and the proprietors' chance of exercising the political means would therefore be precisely nil. Proprietors who made the most profitable exercise of the political means have been those—or rather, speaking strictly, the heirs of those—like the Brevoorts, Wendels, Whitneys, Astors, and Goelets, who owned land in an actual or prospective urban centre, and held it as an investment rather than for speculation.

The lure of the political means in America, however, gave rise to a state of mind which may profitably be examined. Under the feudal State, living by the political means was enabled only by the accident of birth, or in some special cases by the accident of personal favour. Persons outside these categories of accident had no chance whatever to live otherwise than by the economic means. No matter how much they may have wished to exercise the political means, or how greatly they may have envied the privileged few who could exercise it, they were unable to do so; the feudal régime was strictly one of status. Under the merchant-State, on the contrary, the political means was open to anyone, irrespective of birth or position, who had the sagacity and determination necessary to get at it. In this respect, America appeared as a field of unlimited opportunity. The effect of this was to produce a race of people whose master-concern was to avail themselves of this opportunity. They had but the one spring of action, which was the determination to abandon the economic means as soon as they could, and at any sacrifice of conscience or character, and live by the political means. From the beginning, this determination has been universal, amounting to monomania.[10] We need not concern ourselves here with the effect upon the general balance of advantage produced by supplanting the feudal State by the merchant-State; we may observe only that certain virtues and integrities were bred by the régime of status, to which the régime of contract appears to be inimical, even destructive. Vestiges of

[10] It was the ground of Chevalier's observation that Americans had "the morale of an army on the march," and of his equally notable observations on the supreme rule of expediency in America.

them persist among peoples who have had a long experience of the régime of status, but in America, which has had no such experience, they do not appear. What the compensations for their absence may be, or whether they may be regarded as adequate, I repeat, need not concern us; we remark only the simple fact that they have not struck root in the constitution of the American character at large, and apparently can not do so.

II

It was said at the time, I believe, that the actual causes of the colonial revolution of 1776 would never be known. The causes assigned by our schoolbooks may be dismissed as trivial; the various partisan and propagandist views of that struggle and its origins may be put down as incompetent. Great evidential value may be attached to the long line of adverse commercial legislation laid down by the British State from 1651 onward, especially to that portion of it which was enacted after the merchant-State established itself firmly in England in consequence of the events of 1688. This legislation

included the Navigation Acts, the Trade Acts,
acts regulating the colonial currency, the act of
1752 regulating the process of levy and distress,
and the procedures leading up to the establishment of the Board of Trade in 1696.[11] These
directly affected the industrial and commercial
interests in the colonies, though just how seriously is perhaps an open question—enough at
any rate, beyond doubt, to provoke deep resentment.

Over and above these, however, if the reader
will put himself back into the ruling passion of
the time, he will at once appreciate the import
of two matters which have for some reason escaped the attention of historians. The first of
these is the attempt of the British State to limit
the exercise of the political means in respect of
rental-values.[12] In 1763 it forbade the colonists

[11] For a most admirable discussion of these measures and their consequences, cf. Beard, *op. cit.*, vol.
I, pp. 191-220.

[12] In principle, this had been done before; for
example, some of the early royal land-grants reserved
mineral-rights and timber-rights to the Crown. The
Dutch State reserved the right to furs and pelts. Actually, however, these restrictions did not amount to
much, and were not felt as a general grievance, for
these resources had been but little explored.

to take up lands lying westward of the source of any river flowing through the Atlantic seaboard. The dead-line thus established ran so as to cut off from preëmption about half of Pennsylvania and half of Virginia and everything to the west thereof. This was serious. With the mania for speculation running as high as it did, with the consciousness of opportunity, real or fancied, having become so acute and so general, this ruling affected everybody. One can get some idea of its effect by imagining the state of mind of our people at large if stock-gambling had suddenly been outlawed at the beginning of the last great boom in Wall Street a few years ago.

For by this time the colonists had begun to be faintly aware of the illimitable resources of the country lying westward; they had learned just enough about them to fire their imagination and their avarice to a white heat. The seaboard had been pretty well taken up, the free-holding farmer had been pushed back farther and farther, population was coming in steadily, the maritime towns were growing. Under these conditions, "western lands" had become a centre of attraction. Rental-values depended on population, the population was bound to expand, and the one general direction in which it could expand was westward, where lay an immense and incalculably rich domain waiting for preëmption. What could be more natural than that the colonists should itch to get their hands on this territory, and exploit it for themselves alone, and on their own terms, without risk of arbitrary interference by the British State?—and this of necessity meant political independence. It takes no great stress of imagination to see that anyone in those circumstances would have felt that way, and that colonial resentment against the arbitrary limitation which the edict of 1763 put upon the exercise of the political means must therefore have been great.

The actual state of land-speculation during the colonial period will give a fair idea of the probabilities in the case. Most of it was done on the company-system; a number of adventurers would unite, secure a grant of land, survey it, and then sell it off as speedily as they could. Their aim was a quick turnover; they did not, as a rule, contemplate holding the land, much less settling it—in short, their ventures were a pure gamble in rental-values.[13] Among these pre-revolutionary enterprises was the Ohio Company, formed in 1748 with a grant of half a million acres; the Loyal Company, which like the Ohio Company, was composed of Virginians; the Transylvania, the Vandalia, Scioto, Indiana, Wabash, Illinois, Susquehannah, and others whose holdings were smaller.[14] It is interesting to observe the names of persons concerned in these undertakings; one can not escape the significance of this connexion in view of their attitude towards the revolution, and their subsequent career as statesmen and patriots. For example, aside from his individual ventures, General Washington was a member of the Ohio Company, and a prime mover in organizing the Mississippi Company. He also conceived the scheme of the Potomac

[13] There were a few exceptions, but not many; notably in the case of the Wadsworth properties in Western New York, which were held as an investment and leased out on a rental-basis. In one, at least, of General Washington's operations, it appears that he also had this method in view. In 1773 he published an advertisement in a Baltimore newspaper, stating that he had secured a grant of about twenty thousand acres on the Ohio and Kanawha rivers, which he proposed to open to settlers on a rental-basis.

[14] Sakolski, *op. cit.*, ch. I.

Company, which was designed to raise the
rental-value of western holdings by affording
an outlet for their produce by canal and portage
to the Potomac River, and thence to the seaboard. This enterprise determined the establishment of the national capital in its present
most ineligible situation, for the proposed ter-
minus of the canal was at that point. Washington picked up some lots in the city that bears
his name, but in common with other early
speculators, he did not make much money out
of them; they were appraised at about $20,000
when he died.

Patrick Henry was an inveterate and vora-
cious engrosser of land lying beyond the dead-
line set by the British State; later he was heavily
involved in the affairs of one of the notorious
Yazoo companies, operating in Georgia. He
seems to have been most unscrupulous. His
company's holdings in Georgia, amounting to
more than ten million acres, were to be paid
for in Georgia scrip, which was much depreciated. Henry bought up all these certificates
that he could get his hands on, at ten cents on
the dollar, and made a great profit on them by
their rise in value when Hamilton put through

his measure for having the central government assume the debts they represented. Undoubtedly it was this trait of unrestrained avarice which earned him the dislike of Mr. Jefferson, who said, rather contemptuously, that he was "insatiable in money." [15]

Benjamin Franklin's thrifty mind turned cordially to the project of the Vandalia Company, and he acted successfully as promoter for it in England in 1766. Timothy Pickering, who was Secretary of State under Washington and John Adams, went on record in 1796 that "all I am now worth was gained by speculations in land." Silas Deane, emissary of the Continental Congress to France, was interested in the Illinois

[15] It is an odd fact that among the most eminent names of the period, almost the only ones unconnected with land-grabbing or land-jobbing, are those of the two great antagonists, Thomas Jefferson and Alexander Hamilton. Mr. Jefferson had a gentleman's distaste for profiting by any form of the political means; he never even went so far as to patent one of his many useful inventions. Hamilton seems to have cared nothing for money. His measures made many rich, but he never sought anything from them for himself. In general, he appears to have had few scruples, yet amidst the riot of greed and rascality which he did most to promote, he walked worthily. Even his professional fees as a lawyer were absurdly small, and he remained quite poor all his life.

and Wabash Companies, as was Robert Morris, who managed the revolution's finances; as was also James Wilson, who became a justice of the Supreme Court and a mighty man in post-revolutionary land-grabbing. Wolcott of Connecticut, and Stiles, president of Yale College, held stock in the Susquehannah Company; so did Peletiah Webster, Ethan Allen, and Jonathan Trumbull, the "Brother Jonathan," whose name was long a sobriquet for the typical American, and is still sometimes so used. James Duane, the first mayor of New York City, carried on some quite considerable speculative undertakings; and however indisposed one may feel towards entertaining the fact, so did the "Father of the Revolution" himself—Samuel Adams.

A mere common-sense view of the situation would indicate that the British State's interference with a free exercise of the political means was at least as great an incitement to revolution as its interference, through the Navigation Acts, and the Trade Acts, with a free exercise of the economic means. In the nature of things it would be a greater incitement, both because it affected a more numerous class of persons, and because speculation in land-values represented much easier money. Allied with this is the second matter which seems to me deserving of notice, and which has never been properly reckoned with, as far as I know, in studies of the period.

It would seem the most natural thing in the world for the colonists to perceive that independence would not only give freer access to this one mode of the political means, but that it would also open access to other modes which the colonial status made unavailable. The merchant-State existed in the royal provinces complete in structure, but not in function; it did not give access to all the modes of economic exploitation. The advantages of a State which should be wholly autonomous in this respect must have been clear to the colonists, and must have moved them strongly towards the project of establishing one.

Again it is purely a common-sense view of the circumstances that leads to this conclusion. The merchant-State in England had emerged triumphant from conflict, and the colonists had plenty of chance to see what it could do in the way of distributing the various means of eco-

nomic exploitation, and its methods of doing
it. For instance, certain English concerns were
in the carrying trade between England and
America, for which other English concerns
built ships. Americans could compete in both
these lines of business. If they did so, the
carrying-charges would be regulated by the
terms of this competition; if not, they would
be regulated by monopoly, or, in our historic
phrase, they could be set as high as the traffic
would bear. English carriers and shipbuilders
made common cause, approached the State and
asked it to intervene, which it did by for-
bidding the colonists to ship goods on any
but English-built and English-operated ships.
Since freight-charges are a factor in prices, the
effect of this intervention was to enable British
shipowners to pocket the difference between
monopoly-rates and competitive rates; to enable
them, that is, to exploit the consumer by employing the political means.[16] Similar interventions were made at the instance of cutlers,
nailmakers, hatters, steelmakers, etc.

[16] Raw colonial exports were processed in England,
and reëxported to the colonies at prices enhanced in
this way, thus making the political means effective on
the colonists both going and coming.

These interventions took the form of simple prohibition. Another mode of intervention appeared in the customs-duties laid by the British State on foreign sugar and molasses.[17] We all now know pretty well, probably, that the primary reason for a tariff is that it enables the exploitation of the domestic consumer by a process indistinguishable from sheer robbery.[18] All the reasons regularly assigned are debatable; this one is not, hence propagandists and

[17] Beard, *op. cit.*, vol. I, p. 195, cites the observation current in England at the time, that seventy-three members of the Parliament that imposed this tariff were interested in West Indian sugar-plantations.

[18] It must be observed, however, that free trade is impracticable so long as land is kept out of free competition with industry in the labour-market. Discussions of the rival policies of free trade and protection invariably leave this limitation out of account, and are therefore nugatory. Holland and England, commonly spoken of as free-trade countries, were never really such; they had only so much freedom of trade as was consistent with their special economic requirements. American free-traders of the last century, such as Sumner and Godkin, were not really free-traders; they were never able—or willing—to entertain the crucial question why, if free trade is a good thing, the conditions of labour were no better in free-trade England than, for instance, in protectionist Germany, but were in fact worse. The answer is, of course, that England had no unpreëmpted land to absorb displaced labour, or to stand in continuous competition with industry for labour.

lobbyists never mention it. The colonists were well aware of this reason, and the best evidence that they were aware of it is that long before the Union was established, the merchant-enter-prisers and industrialists were ready and wait-ing to set upon the new-formed administra-tion with an organized demand for a tariff.

It is clear that while in the nature of things the British State's interventions upon the eco-nomic means would stir up great resentment among the interests directly concerned, they would have another effect fully as significant, if not more so, in causing those interests to look favourably on the idea of political independ-ence. They could hardly have helped seeing the positive as well as the negative advantage that would accrue from setting up a State of their own, which they might bend to their own purposes. It takes no great amount of imagina-tion to reconstruct the vision that appeared before them of a merchant-State clothed with full powers of intervention and discrimination, a State which should first and last "help busi-ness," and which should be administered either by mere agents or by persons easily manageable, if not by persons of actual interests like to their own. It is hardly presumable that the colonists generally were not intelligent enough to see this vision, or that they were not resolute enough to risk the chance of realizing it when the time could be made ripe; as it was, the time was ripened almost before it was ready.[19] We can discern a distinct line of common purpose uniting the interests of the merchant-enterpriser with those of the actual or potential speculator in rental-values—uniting the Hancocks, Gores, Otises, with the Henrys, Lees, Wolcotts, Trumbulls—and leading directly towards the goal of political independence.

The main conclusion, however, towards which these observations tend, is that one general frame of mind existed among the colonists with reference to the nature and primary function of the State. This frame of mind was not peculiar to them; they shared it with the beneficiaries of the merchant-State in England, and with those of the feudal State as far back as the

[19] The immense amount of labour involved in getting the revolution going, and keeping it going, is not as yet exactly a commonplace of American history, but it has begun to be pretty well understood, and the various myths about it have been exploded by the researches of disinterested historians.

State's history can be traced. Voltaire, sur-
veying the débris of the feudal State, said that
in essence the State is "a device for taking
money out of one set of pockets and putting it
into another." The beneficiaries of the feudal
State had precisely this view, and they be-
queathed it unchanged and unmodified to the
actual and potential beneficiaries of the merchant-State. The colonists regarded the State
as primarily an instrument whereby one might
help oneself and hurt others; that is to say, first
and foremost they regarded it as the organization of the political means. No other view of
the State was ever held in colonial America.
Romance and poetry were brought to bear on
the subject in the customary way; glamorous
myths about it were propagated with the customary intent; but when all came to all, nowhere in colonial America were actual practical
relations with the State ever determined by any
other view than this.[20]

[20] The influence of this view upon the rise of nationalism and the maintenance of the national spirit
in the modern world, now that the merchant-State
has so generally superseded the feudal State, may be
perceived at once. I do not think it has ever been
thoroughly discussed, or that the sentiment of patriotism has ever been thoroughly examined for traces of

III

The charter of the American revolution was the Declaration of Independence, which took its stand on the double thesis of "unalienable" natural rights and popular sovereignty. We have seen that these doctrines were theoretically, or as politicians say, "in principle," congenial to the spirit of the English merchant-enterpriser, and we may see that in the nature of things they would be even more agreeable to the spirit of all classes in American society. A thin and scattered population with a whole wide world before it, with a vast territory full of rich resources which anyone might take a hand at preëmpting and exploiting, would be strongly on the side of natural rights, as the colonists were from the beginning; and political independence would confirm it in that position. These circumstances would stiffen the American merchant-enterpriser, agrarian, forestaller and industrialist alike in a jealous, uncompromising, and assertive economic individualism.

this view, though one might suppose that such a work would be extremely useful.

So also with the sister doctrine of popular sovereignty. The colonists had been through a long and vexatious experience of State interventions which limited their use of both the political and economic means. They had also been given plenty of opportunity to see how these interventions had been managed, and how the interested English economic groups which did the managing had profited at their expense. Hence there was no place in their minds for any political theory that disallowed the right of individual self-expression in politics. As their situation tended to make them natural-born economic individualists, so also it tended to make them natural-born republicans.

Thus the preamble of the Declaration hit the mark of a cordial unanimity. Its two leading doctrines could easily be interpreted as justifying an unlimited economic pseudo-individualism on the part of the State's beneficiaries, and a judiciously managed exercise of political self-expression by the electorate. Whether or not this were a more free-and-easy interpretation than a strict construction of the doctrines will bear, no doubt it was in effect the interpretation quite commonly put upon them. American history abounds in instances where great principles have, in their common understanding and practical application, been narrowed down to the service of very paltry ends. The preamble, nevertheless, did reflect a general state of mind. However incompetent the understanding of its doctrines may have been, and however interested the motives which prompted that understanding, the general spirit of the people was in their favour.

There was complete unanimity also regarding the nature of the new and independent political institution which the Declaration contemplated as within "the right of the people" to set up. There was a great and memorable dissension about its form, but none about its nature. It should be in essence the mere continuator of the merchant-State already existing. There was no idea of setting up *government,* the purely social institution which should have no other object than, as the Declaration put it, to secure the natural rights of the individual; or as Paine put it, which should contemplate nothing beyond the maintenance of freedom and security—the institution which should make no positive interventions of any kind upon the

individual, but should confine itself exclusively
to such negative interventions as the maintenance of freedom and security might indicate.
The idea was to perpetuate an institution of
another character entirely, *the State,* the organization of the political means; and this was accordingly done.

There is no disparagement implied in this
observation; for, all questions of motive aside,
nothing else was to be expected. No one knew
any other kind of political organization. The
causes of American complaint were conceived
of as due only to interested and culpable mal-
administration, not to the essentially anti-social
nature of the institution administered. Dissatisfaction was directed against administrators,
not against the institution itself. Violent dislike of the *form* of the institution—the monarchical form—was engendered, but no distrust
or suspicion of its nature. The character of
the State had never been subjected to scrutiny;
the coöperation of the *Zeitgeist* was needed for
that, and it was not yet to be had.[21] One may

[21] Even now its coöperation seems not to have got
very far in English and American professional circles.
The latest English exponent of the State, Professor
Laski, draws the same set of elaborate distinctions

see here a parallel with the revolutionary movements against the Church in the sixteenth century—and indeed with revolutionary movements in general. They are incited by abuses
and misfeasances, more or less specific and always secondary, and are carried on with no idea
beyond getting them rectified or avenged,
usually by the sacrifice of conspicuous scape-
goats. The philosophy of the institution that
gives play to these misfeasances is never examined, and hence they recur promptly under
another form or other auspices,[22] or else their
place is taken by others which are in character
precisely like them. Thus the notorious failure
of reforming and revolutionary movements in
the long-run may as a rule be found due to their
incorrigible superficiality.

One mind, indeed, came within reaching distance of the fundamentals of the matter, not by

between the State and officialdom that one would
look for if he had been writing a hundred and fifty
years ago. He appears to regard the State as essentially a social institution, though his observations on
this point are by no means clear. Since his conclusions tend towards collectivism, however, the infer-
ence seems admissible.

[22] As, for example, when one political party is
turned out of office, and another put in.

employing the historical method, but by a
homespun kind of reasoning, aided by a sound
and sensitive instinct. The common view of
Mr. Jefferson as a doctrinaire believer in the
stark principle of "states' rights" is most incompetent and misleading. He believed in
states' rights, assuredly, but he went much
farther; states' rights were only an incident in
his general system of political organization.
He believed that the ultimate political unit,
the repository and source of political authority
and initiative, should be the smallest unit; not
the federal unit, state unit or county unit, but
the township, or, as he called it, the "ward."
The township, and the township only, should
determine the delegation of power upwards to
the county, the state, and the federal units. His
system of extreme decentralization is interesting and perhaps worth a moment's examination,
because if the idea of *the State* is ever displaced
by the idea of *government*, it seems probable
that the practical expression of this idea would
come out very nearly in that form.[23] There is

[23] In fact, the only modification of it that one can
foresee as necessary is that the smallest unit should
reserve the taxing-power strictly to itself. The larger
units should have no power whatever of direct or

probably no need to say that the consideration of such a displacement involves a long look ahead, and over a field of view that is cluttered with the débris of a most discouraging number, not of nations alone, but of whole civilizations. Nevertheless it is interesting to remind ourselves that more than a hundred and fifty years ago, one American succeeded in getting below the surface of things, and that he probably to some degree anticipated the judgment of an immeasurably distant future.

In February, 1816, Mr. Jefferson wrote a letter to Joseph C. Cabell, in which he expounded the philosophy behind his system of political organization. What is it, he asks, that has "de-

indirect taxation, but should present their requirements to the townships, to be met by quota. This would tend to reduce the organizations of the larger units to skeleton form, and would operate strongly against their assuming any functions but those assigned them, which under a strictly governmental régime would be very few—for the federal unit, indeed, extremely few. It is interesting to imagine the suppression of every bureaucratic activity in Washington today that has to do with the maintenance and administration of the political means, and see how little would be left. If the State were superseded by government, probably every federal activity could be housed in the Senate Office Building—quite possibly with room to spare.

stroyed liberty and the rights of man in every
government which has ever existed under the
sun? The generalizing and concentrating all
cares and powers into one body, no matter
whether of the autocrats of Russia or France, or
of the aristocrats of a Venetian senate." The
secret of freedom will be found in the individual "making himself the depository of the
powers respecting himself, so far as he is competent to them, and delegating only what is
beyond his competence, by a synthetical process, to higher and higher orders of function-
aries, so as to trust fewer and fewer powers in
proportion as the trustees become more and
more oligarchical." This idea rests on accurate
observation, for we are all aware that not only
the wisdom of the ordinary man, but also his
interest and sentiment, have a very short radius
of operation; they can not be stretched over an
area of much more than township-size; and it
is the acme of absurdity to suppose that any
man or any body of men can arbitrarily exercise their wisdom, interest and sentiment over
a state-wide or nation-wide area with any kind
of success. Therefore the principle must hold
that the larger the area of exercise, the fewer

and more clearly defined should be the functions exercised. Moreover, "by placing under everyone what his own eye may superintend," there is erected the surest safeguard against usurpation of function. "Where every man is a sharer in the direction of his ward-republic, or of some of the higher ones, and feels that he is a participator in the government of affairs, not merely at an election one day in the year, but every day; . . . he will let the heart be torn out of his body sooner than his power wrested from him by a Cæsar or a Bonaparte."

No such idea of popular sovereignty, however, appeared in the political organization that was set up in 1789—far from it. In devising their structure, the American architects followed certain specifications laid down by Harington, Locke and Adam Smith, which might be regarded as a sort of official digest of politics under the merchant-State; indeed, if one wished to be perhaps a little inurbane in describing them—though not actually unjust—one might say that they are the merchant-State's defence-mechanism.[24]   Harington laid down the all-

[24] Harington published the *Oceana* in 1656. Locke's political treatises were published in 1690. Smith's

important principle that the basis of politics is
economic—that power follows property. Since
he was arguing against the feudal concept, he
laid stress specifically upon landed property.
He was of course too early to perceive the bear-
ings of the State-system of land-tenure upon
industrial exploitation, and neither he nor
Locke perceived any natural distinction to be
drawn between law-made property and labour-
made property; nor yet did Smith perceive this
clearly, though he seems to have had occasional
indistinct glimpses of it. According to Harington's theory of economic determinism, the reali-
zation of popular sovereignty is a simple matter.
Since political power proceeds from land-ownership, a simple diffusion of land-ownership is
all that is needed to insure a satisfactory distribution of power.[25] If everybody owns, then
everybody rules. "If the people hold three

*Inquiry into the Nature and Causes of the Wealth
of Nations* appeared in 1776.

[25] This theory, with its corollary that democracy is
primarily an economic rather than a political status,
is extremely modern. The Physiocrats in France, and
Henry George in America, modified Harington's practical proposals by showing that the same results could
be obtained by the more convenient method of a
local confiscation of economic rent.

parts in four of the territory," Harington says, "it is plain there can neither be any single person nor nobility able to dispute the government with them. In this case therefore, except force be interposed, they govern themselves."

Locke, writing a half-century later, when the revolution of 1688 was over, concerned himself more particularly with the State's positive confiscatory interventions upon other modes of property-ownership. These had long been frequent and vexatious, and under the Stuarts they had amounted to unconscionable highwaymanry. Locke's idea therefore was to copper-rivet such a doctrine of the sacredness of property as would forever put a stop to this sort of thing. Hence he laid it down that the first business of the State is to maintain the absolute inviolability of general property-rights; the State itself might not violate them, because in so doing it would act against its own primary function. Thus in Locke's view, the rights of property took precedence even over those of life and liberty; and if ever it came to the pinch, the State must make its choice accordingly.[26]

[26] Locke held that in time of war it was competent for the State to conscript the lives and liberties of its

Thus while the American architects assented
"in principle" to the philosophy of natural
rights and popular sovereignty, and found it
in a general way highly congenial as a sort of
voucher for their self-esteem, their practical
interpretation of it left it pretty well ham-
strung. They were not especially concerned
with consistency; their practical interest in this
philosophy stopped short at the point which we
have already noted, of its presumptive justification of a ruthless economic pseudo-individualism, and an exercise of political self-expression by the general electorate which should be
so managed as to be, in all essential respects,
futile. In this they took precise pattern by the
English Whig exponents and practitioners of
this philosophy. Locke himself, whom we

subjects, but not their property. It is interesting to
remark the persistence of this view in the practice of
the merchant-State at the present time. In the last
great collision of competing interests among mer-
chant-States, twenty years ago, the State everywhere
intervened at wholesale upon the rights of life and
liberty, but was very circumspect towards the rights
of property. Since the principle of absolutism was
introduced into our constitution by the income-tax
amendment, several attempts have been made to reduce the rights of property, in time of war, to an
approximately equal footing with those of life and
liberty; but so far, without success.

have seen putting the natural rights of property
so high above those of life and liberty, was
equally discriminating in his view of popular
sovereignty. He was no believer in what he
called "a numerous democracy," and did not
contemplate a political organization that
should countenance anything of the kind.[27]
The sort of organization he had in mind is reflected in the extraordinary constitution he de-
vised for the royal province of Carolina, which
established a basic order of politically inarticu-
late serfdom. Such an organization as this

[27] It is worth going through the literature of the
late seventeenth and early eighteenth century to see
how the words "democracy" and "democrat" appear
exclusively as terms of contumely and reprehension.
They served this purpose for a long time both in England and America, much as the terms "bolshevism"
and "bolshevist" serve us now. They were subsequently taken over to become what Bentham called
"impostor-terms," in behalf of the existing economic
and political order, as synonymous with a purely
nominal republicanism. They are now used regularly in this way to describe the political system of
the United States, even by persons who should know
better—even, curiously, by persons like Bertrand Rus-
sell and Mr. Laski, who have little sympathy with the
existing order. One sometimes wonders how our
revolutionary forefathers would take it if they could
hear some flatulent political thimblerigger charge
them with having founded "the great and glorious
democracy of the West."

represented about the best, in a practical way, that the British merchant-State was ever able to do for the doctrine of popular sovereignty.

It was also about the best that the American counterpart of the British merchant-State could do. The sum of the matter is that while the philosophy of natural rights and popular sovereignty afforded a set of principles upon which all interests could unite, and practically all did unite, with the aim of securing political independence, it did not afford a satisfactory set of principles on which to found the new American State. When political independence was secured, the stark doctrine of the Declaration went into abeyance, with only a distorted simulacrum of its principles surviving. The rights of life and liberty were recognized by a mere constitutional formality left open to eviscerating interpretations, or, where these were for any reason deemed superfluous, to simple executive disregard; and all consideration of the rights attending "the pursuit of happiness" was narrowed down to a plenary acceptance of Locke's doctrine of the preëminent rights of property, with law-made property on an equal footing with labour-made property. As for popular sovereignty, the new State had to be republican in form, for no other would suit the general temper of the people; and hence its peculiar task was to preserve the appearance of actual republicanism without the reality.   To do this, it took over the apparatus which we have seen the English merchant-State adopting when confronted with a like task—the apparatus of a representative or parliamentary system. Moreover, it improved upon the British model of this apparatus by adding three auxiliary devices which time has proved most effective. These were, first, the device of the fixed term, which regulates the administration of our system by astronomical rather than political considerations—by the motion of the earth around the sun rather than by political exigency; second, the device of judicial review and interpretation, which, as we have already observed, is a process whereby anything may be made to mean anything; third, the device of requiring legislators to reside in the district they represent, which puts the highest conceivable premium upon pliancy and venality, and is therefore the best mechanism for rapidly building up an immense body of patronage.   It may be perceived at once that all these devices tend of themselves to work smoothly and harmoniously towards a great centralization of State power, and that their working in this direction may be indefinitely accelerated with the utmost economy of effort.

As well as one can put a date to such an event, the surrender at Yorktown marks the sudden and complete disappearance of the Declaration's doctrine from the political consciousness of America. Mr. Jefferson resided in Paris as minister to France from 1784 to 1789. As the time for his return to America drew near, he wrote Colonel Humphreys that he hoped soon "to possess myself anew, by conversation with my countrymen, of their spirit and ideas. I know only the Americans of the year 1784. They tell me this is to be much a stranger to those of 1789." So indeed he found it. On arriving in New York and resuming his place in the social life of the country, he was greatly depressed by the discovery that the principles of the Declaration had gone wholly by the board. No one spoke of natural rights and popular sovereignty; it would seem actually that no one had ever heard of them. On the contrary, everyone was talking about the pressing need of a strong central coercive authority, able to check the incursions which "the democratic spirit" was likely to incite upon "the men of principle and property." [28] Mr. Jefferson wrote despondently of the contrast of all this with the sort of thing he had been hearing in the France which he had just left "in the first year of her revolution, in the fervour of natural rights and zeal for reformation." In the process of possessing himself anew of the spirit and ideas of his countrymen, he said, "I can not describe the wonder and mortification with which the table-conversations filled me." Clearly, though the Declaration might have been the charter of American independence, it was in no sense the charter of the new American State.

[28] This curious collocation of attributes belongs to General Henry Knox, Washington's secretary of war, and a busy speculator in land-values. He used it in a letter to Washington, on the occasion of Shays's Rebellion in 1786, in which he made an agonized plea for a strong federal army. In the literature of the period, it is interesting to observe how regularly a moral superiority is associated with the possession of property.

5

IT IS a commonplace that the persistence of an institution is due solely to the state of mind that prevails towards it, the set of terms in which men habitually think about it. So long, and only so long, as those terms are favourable, the institution lives and maintains its power; and when for any reason men generally cease thinking in those terms, it weakens and becomes inert. At one time, a certain set of terms regarding man's place in nature gave organized Christianity the power largely to control men's consciences and direct their conduct; and this power has dwindled to the point of disappearance, for no other reason than that men generally stopped thinking in those terms. The persistence of our unstable and iniquitous economic system is not due to the power of accumulated capital, the force of propaganda, or to any force or combination of forces commonly alleged as its cause. It is due solely to a certain set of terms in which men think of the opportunity to work; they regard this opportunity as something to be *given*. Nowhere is there any other idea about it than that the opportunity to apply labour and capital to natural resources for the production of wealth is not in any sense a right, but a concession.[1] This is all that keeps our system alive. When men cease to think in those terms, the system will disappear, and not before.

It seems pretty clear that changes in the terms of thought affecting an institution are but little advanced by direct means. They are brought about in obscure and circuitous ways, and assisted by trains of circumstance which before the fact would appear quite unrelated, and their erosive or solvent action is therefore quite unpredictable. A direct drive at effect-

[1] Consider, for example, the present situation. Our natural resources, while much depleted, are still great; our population is very thin, running something like twenty or twenty-five to the square mile; and some millions of this population are at the moment "unemployed," and likely to remain so because no one will or can "give them work." The point is not that men generally submit to this state of things, or that they accept it as inevitable, but that they see nothing irregular or anomalous about it because of their fixed idea that work is something to be *given*.

ing these changes comes as a rule to nothing, or more often than not turns out to be retarding. They are so largely the work of those unimpassioned and imperturbable agencies for which Prince de Bismarck had such vast respect—he called them the *imponderabilia*—that any effort which disregards them, or thrusts them violently aside, will in the longrun find them stepping in to abort its fruit.

Thus it is that what we are attempting to do in this rapid survey of the historical progress of certain ideas, is to trace the genesis of an attitude of mind, a set of terms in which now practically everyone thinks of the State; and then to consider the conclusions towards which this psychical phenomenon unmistakably points. Instead of recognizing the State as "the common enemy of all well-disposed, industrious and decent men," the run of mankind, with rare exceptions, regards it not only as a final and indispensable entity, but also as, in the main, beneficent. The mass-man, ignorant of its history, regards its character and intentions as social rather than anti-social; and in that faith he is willing to put at its disposal an indefinite credit of knavery, mendacity and chi-

cane, upon which its administrators may draw
at will. Instead of looking upon the State's
progressive absorption of social power with the
repugnance and resentment that he would
naturally feel towards the activities of a professional-criminal organization, he tends rather to
encourage and glorify it, in the belief that he is
somehow identified with the State, and that
therefore, in consenting to its indefinite aggrandizement, he consents to something in
which he has a share—he is, *pro tanto*, aggran-
dizing himself. Professor Ortega y Gasset
analyzes this state of mind extremely well. The
mass-man, he says, confronting the phenomenon of the State, "sees it, admires it, knows
that *there it is.* . . . Furthermore, the mass-
man sees in the State an anonymous power, and
feeling himself, like it, anonymous, he believes
that the State is something of his own. Suppose that in the public life of a country some
difficulty, conflict, or problem, presents itself,
the mass-man will tend to demand that the
State intervene immediately and undertake a
solution directly with its immense and unas-
sailable resources. . . . When the mass suffers
any ill-fortune, or simply feels some strong ap-

petite, its great temptation is that permanent sure possibility of obtaining everything, without effort, struggle, doubt, or risk, merely by touching a button and setting the mighty machine in motion."

It is the genesis of this attitude, this state of mind, and the conclusions which inexorably follow from its predominance, that we are attempting to get at through our present survey. These conclusions may perhaps be briefly forecast here, in order that the reader who is for any reason indisposed to entertain them may take warning of them at this point, and close the book.

The unquestioning, determined, even truculent maintenance of the attitude which Professor Ortega y Gasset so admirably describes, is obviously the life and strength of the State; and obviously too, it is now so inveterate and so wide-spread—one may freely call it universal—that no direct effort could overcome its inveteracy or modify it, and least of all hope to enlighten it. This attitude can only be sapped and mined by uncountable generations of experience, in a course marked by recurrent calamity of a most appalling character. When once the predominance of this attitude in any given civilization has become inveterate, as so plainly it has become in the civilization of America, all that can be done is to leave it to work its own way out to its appointed end. The philosophic historian may content himself with pointing out and clearly elucidating its consequences, as Professor Ortega y Gasset has done, aware that after this there is no more that one can do. "The result of this tendency," he says, "will be fatal. Spontaneous social action will be broken up over and over again by State intervention; no new seed will be able to fructify.[2] Society will have to live *for* the State, man *for* the governmental machine. And as after all it is only a machine, whose existence and maintenance depend on the vital supports around it,[3] the State, after sucking out the very

[2] The present paralysis of production, for example, is due solely to State intervention, and uncertainty concerning further intervention.

[3] It seems to be very imperfectly understood that the cost of State intervention must be paid out of production, this being the only source from which any payment for anything can be derived. Intervention retards production; then the resulting stringency and inconvenience enable further intervention, which in turn still further retards production; and this process goes on until, as in Rome, in the third cen-

marrow of society, will be left bloodless, a skeleton, dead with that rusty death of machinery, more gruesome than the death of a living organism. Such was the lamentable fate of ancient civilization."

II

The revolution of 1776-1781 converted thirteen provinces, practically as they stood, into thirteen autonomous political units, completely independent, and they so continued until 1789, formally held together as a sort of league, by the Articles of Confederation. For our purposes, the point to be remarked about this eight-year period, 1781-1789, is that administration of the political means was not centralized in the federation, but in the several units of which the federation was composed. The federal assembly, or congress, was hardly more than a deliberative body of delegates appointed by the autonomous units. It had no taxing-power, and no coercive power. It could not command funds for any enterprise common to

tury, production ceases entirely, and the source of payment dries up.

the federation, even for war; all it could do was to apportion the sum needed, in the hope that each unit would meet its quota. There was no coercive federal authority over these matters, or over any matters; the sovereignty of each of the thirteen federated units was complete.

Thus the central body of this loose association of sovereignties had nothing to say about the distribution of the political means. This authority was vested in the several component units. Each unit had absolute jurisdiction over its territorial basis, and could partition it as it saw fit, and could maintain any system of land-tenure that it chose to establish.[4] Each unit set up its own trade-regulations. Each unit levied its own tariffs, one against another, in behalf of its own chosen beneficiaries. Each manufactured its own currency, and might manipulate it as it liked, for the benefit of such individuals or economic groups as were able to get effective access to the local legislature.

[4] As a matter of fact, all thirteen units merely continued the system that had existed throughout the colonial period—the system which gave the beneficiary a monopoly of rental-values as well as a monopoly of use-values. No other system was ever known in America, except in the short-lived state of Deseret, under the Mormon polity.

Each managed its own system of bounties, concessions, subsidies, franchises, and exercised it with a view to whatever private interest its legislature might be influenced to promote. In short, the whole mechanism of the political means was non-national. The federation was not in any sense a State; the State was not one, but thirteen.

Within each unit, therefore, as soon as the war was over, there began at once a general scramble for access to the political means. It must never be forgotten that in each unit society was fluid; this access was available to anyone gifted with the peculiar sagacity and resolution necessary to get at it. Hence one economic interest after another brought pressure of influence to bear on the local legislatures, until the economic hand of every unit was against every other, and the hand of every other was against itself. The principle of "protection," which as we have seen was already well understood, was carried to lengths precisely comparable with those to which it is carried in international commerce today, and for precisely the same primary purpose—the exploitation, or in plain terms the robbery, of the domestic consumer. Mr. Beard remarks that the legislature of New York, for example, pressed the principle which governs tariff-making to the point of levying duties on firewood brought in from Connecticut and on cabbages from New Jersey —a fairly close parallel with the *octroi* that one still encounters at the gates of French towns.

The primary monopoly, fundamental to all others—the monopoly of economic rent—was sought with redoubled eagerness.[5] The territorial basis of each unit now included the vast holdings confiscated from British owners, and the bar erected by the British State's proclamation of 1763 against the appropriation of Western lands was now removed. Professor Sakolski observes drily that "the early land-lust which the colonists inherited from their European forebears was not diminished by the democratic spirit of the revolutionary fathers." Indeed not! Land-grants were sought as assiduously from local legislatures as they had been in earlier days from the Stuart dynasty and from colonial governors, and the mania of land-jobbing ran apace with the mania of land-

[5] For a brilliant summary of post-revolutionary land-speculation, cf. Sakolski, *op. cit.,* ch. II.

grabbing.[6] Among the men most actively interested in these pursuits were those whom we
have already seen identified with them in pre-
revolutionary days, such as the two Morrises,
Knox, Pickering, James Wilson and Patrick
Henry; and with their names appear those of
Duer, Bingham, McKean, Willing, Greenleaf,
Nicholson, Aaron Burr, Low, Macomb, Wadsworth, Remsen, Constable, Pierrepont, and
others which now are less well remembered.

There is probably no need to follow out the
rather repulsive trail of effort after other modes
of the political means. What we have said

[6] Mr. Sakolski very justly remarks that the mania
for land-jobbing was stimulated by the action of the
new units in offering lands by way of settlement of
their public debts, which led to extensive gambling
in the various issues of "land-warrants." The list of
eminent names involved in this enterprise includes
Wilson C. Nicholas, who later became governor of
Virginia; "Light Horse Harry" Lee, father of the
great Confederate commander; General John Preston,
of Smithfield; and George Taylor, brother-in-law of
Chief Justice Marshall. Lee, Preston and Nicholas
were prosecuted at the instance of some Connecticut
speculators, for a transaction alleged as fraudulent;
Lee was arrested in Boston, on the eve of embarking
for the West Indies. They had deeded a tract, said
to be of 300,000 acres, at ten cents an acre, but on
being surveyed, the tract did not come to half that
size. Frauds of this order were extremely common.

about the foregoing two modes—tariffs and rental-value monopoly—is doubtless enough to illustrate satisfactorily the spirit and attitude of mind towards the State during the eight years immediately following the revolution. The whole story of insensate scuffle for State-created economic advantage is not especially animating, nor is it essential to our purposes. Such as it is, it may be read in detail elsewhere. All that interests us is to observe that during the eight years of federation, the principles of government set forth by Paine and by the Declaration continued in utter abeyance. Not only did the philosophy of natural rights and popular sovereignty [7] remain as completely out of consideration as when Mr. Jefferson first lamented its disappearance, but the idea of government as a social institution based on this philosophy was likewise unconsidered. No one thought of a political organization as instituted "to secure these rights" by processes of purely negative

[7] The new political units continued the colonial practice of restricting the suffrage to taxpayers and owners of property, and none but men of considerable wealth were eligible to public office. Thus the exercise of sovereignty was a matter of economic right, not natural right.

intervention—instituted, that is, with no other
end in view than the maintenance of "freedom
and security."   The history of the eight-year
period of federation shows no trace whatever of
any idea of political organization other than the
State-idea.   No one regarded this organization
otherwise than as the organization of the political means, an all-powerful engine which
should stand permanently ready and available
for the irresistible promotion of this-or-that set
of economic interests, and the irremediable disservice of others; according as whichever set,
by whatever course of strategy, might succeed
in obtaining command of its machinery.

III

It may be repeated that while State power
was well centralized under the federation, it
was not centralized in the federation, but in the
federated unit.   For various reasons, some of
them plausible, many leading citizens, especially in the more northerly units, found this
distribution of power unsatisfactory; and a considerable compact group of economic interests
which stood to profit by a redistribution natu-

rally made the most of these reasons. It is quite
certain that dissatisfaction with the existing ar-
rangement was not general, for when the redistribution took place in 1789, it was effected
with great difficulty and only through a *coup
d'État,* organized by methods which if employed
in any other field than that of politics, would
be put down at once as not only daring, but
unscrupulous and dishonourable.

The situation, in a word, was that American
economic interests had fallen into two grand
divisions, the special interests in each having
made common cause with a view to capturing
control of the political means. One division
comprised the speculating, industrial-commer-
cial and creditor interests, with their natural
allies of the bar and bench, the pulpit and the
press. The other comprised chiefly the farmers
and artisans and the debtor class generally.
From the first, these two grand divisions were
colliding briskly here and there in the several
units, the most serious collision occurring over
the terms of the Massachusetts constitution of
1780.[8] The State in each of the thirteen units

[8] This was the uprising known as Shays's Rebellion,
which took place in 1786. The creditor division in

was a class-State, as every State known to history
has been; and the work of manœuvring it in
its function of enabling the economic exploitation of one class by another went steadily on.

General conditions under the Articles of
Confederation were pretty good.   The people

Massachusetts had gained control of the political
means, and had fortified its control by establishing
a constitution which was made to bear so hardly on
the agrarian and debtor division that an armed insurrection broke out six years later, led by Daniel
Shays, for the purpose of annulling its onerous provisions, and transferring control of the political means
to the latter group.   This incident affords a striking
view in miniature of the State's nature and teleology.
The rebellion had a great effect in consolidating the
creditor division and giving plausibility to its contention for the establishment of a strong coercive
national State.   Mr. Jefferson spoke contemptuously
of this contention, as "the interested clamours and
sophistry of speculating, shaving and banking institutions"; and of the rebellion itself he observed to
Mrs. John Adams, whose husband had most to do
with drafting the Massachusetts constitution, "I like
a little rebellion now and then. . . . The spirit of
resistance to government is so valuable that I wish
it to be always kept alive.   It will often be exercised
when wrong, but better so than not to be exercised
at all."   Writing to another correspondent at the
same time, he said earnestly, "God forbid we should
ever be twenty years without such a rebellion."
Obiter dicta of this nature, scattered here and there
in Mr. Jefferson's writings, have the interest of showing how near his instinct led him towards a clear
understanding of the State's character.

had made a creditable recovery from the dislocations and disturbances due to the revolution, and there was a very decent prospect that
Mr. Jefferson's idea of a political organization
which should be national in foreign affairs and
non-national in domestic affairs might be found
continuously practicable. Some tinkering with
the Articles seemed necessary—in fact, it was
expected—but nothing that would transform or
seriously impair the general scheme. The chief
trouble was with the federation's weakness in
view of the chance of war, and in respect of
debts due to foreign creditors. The Articles,
however, carried provision for their own
amendment, and for anything one can see, such
amendment as the general scheme made necessary was quite feasible. In fact, when sugges-
tions of revision arose, as they did almost immediately, nothing else appears to have been
contemplated.

But the general scheme itself was as a whole
objectionable to the interests grouped in the
first grand division. The grounds of their dissatisfaction are obvious enough. When one
bears in mind the vast prospect of the con-
tinent, one need use but little imagination to

perceive that the national scheme was by far
the more congenial to those interests, because
it enabled an ever-closer centralization of control over the political means. For instance,
leaving aside the advantage of having but one
central tariff-making body to chaffer with, instead of twelve, any industrialist could see the
great primary advantage of being able to extend
his exploiting operations over a nation-wide
free-trade area walled-in by a general tariff;
the closer the centralization, the larger the exploitable area. Any speculator in rental-values
would be quick to see the advantage of bringing
this form of opportunity under unified control.[9]
Any speculator in depreciated public securities
would be strongly for a system that could offer
him the use of the political means to bring back
their face-value.[10]   Any shipowner or foreign

[9] Professor Sakolski observes that after the Articles
of Confederation were supplanted by the constitution, schemes of land-speculation "multiplied with
renewed and intensified energy." Naturally so, for
as he says, the new scheme of a national State got
strong support from this class of adventurers because
they foresaw that rental-values "must be greatly in-
creased by an efficient federal government."

[10] More than half the delegates to the constitutional
convention of 1787 were either investors or speculators in the public funds. Probably sixty per cent

trader would be quick to see that his bread was buttered on the side of a national State which, if properly approached, might lend him the use of the political means by way of a subsidy, or would be able to back up some profitable but dubious freebooting enterprise with "diplomatic representations" or with reprisals.

The farmers and the debtor class in general, on the other hand, were not interested in these considerations, but were strongly for letting things stay, for the most part, as they stood. Preponderance in the local legislatures gave them satisfactory control of the political means, which they could and did use to the prejudice of the creditor class, and they did not care to be disturbed in their preponderance. They were agreeable to such modification of the Articles as should work out short of this, but not to setting up a national [11] replica of the British

of the values represented by these securities were fictitious, and were so regarded even by their holders.

[11] It may be observed that at this time the word "national" was a term of obloquy, carrying somewhat the same implications that the word "fascist" carries in some quarters today. Nothing is more interesting than the history of political terms in their relation to the shifting balance of economic advantage—except, perhaps, the history of the partisan movements which they designate, viewed in the same relation.

merchant-State, which they perceived was precisely what the classes grouped in the opposing grand division wished to do. These classes aimed at bringing in the British system of economics, politics and judicial control, on a nation-wide scale; and the interests grouped in the second division saw that what this would really come to was a shifting of the incidence of economic exploitation upon themselves. They had an impressive object-lesson in the immediate shift that took place in Massachusetts after the adoption of John Adams's local constitution of 1780. They naturally did not care to see this sort of thing put into operation on a nation-wide scale, and they therefore looked with extreme disfavour upon any bait put forth for amending the Articles out of existence. When Hamilton, in 1780, objected to the Articles in the form in which they were proposed for adoption, and proposed the calling of a constitutional convention instead, they turned the cold shoulder; as they did again to Washington's letter to the local governors three years later, in which he adverted to the need of a strong coercive central authority.

Finally, however, a constitutional convention

was assembled, on the distinct understanding that it should do no more than revise the Articles in such a way, as Hamilton cleverly phrased it, as to make them "adequate to the exigencies of the nation," and on the further understanding that all the thirteen units should assent to the amendments before they went into effect; in short, that the method of amendment provided by the Articles themselves should be followed. Neither understanding was fulfilled. The convention was made up wholly of men representing the economic interests of the first division. The great majority of them, possibly as many as four-fifths, were public creditors; one-third were land-speculators; some were money-lenders; one-fifth were industrialists, traders, shippers; and many of them were lawyers. They planned and executed a *coup d'État,* simply tossing the Articles of Confederation into the waste-basket, and drafting a constitution *de novo,* with the audacious provision that it should go into effect when ratified by nine units instead of by all thirteen. Moreover, with like audacity, they provided that the document should not be submitted either to the

Congress or to the local legislatures, but that it should go direct to a popular vote! [12]

The unscrupulous methods employed in securing ratification need not be dwelt on here.[13] We are not indeed concerned with the moral quality of any of the proceedings by which the constitution was brought into being, but only with showing their instrumentality in encouraging a definite general idea of the State and its functions, and a consequent general attitude towards the State. We therefore go on to observe that in order to secure ratification by even the nine necessary units, the document had to conform to certain very exacting and difficult requirements. The political structure which it contemplated had to be republican in form, yet capable of resisting what Gerry unctuously called "the excess of democracy," and what

[12] The obvious reason for this, as the event showed, was that the interests grouped in the first division had the advantage of being relatively compact and easily mobilized. Those in the second division, being chiefly agrarian, were loose and sprawling, communications among them were slow, and mobilization difficult.

[13] They have been noticed by several recent authorities, and are exhibited fully in Mr. Beard's monumental *Economic Interpretation of the Constitution of the United States.*

Randolph termed its "turbulence and follies."
The task of the delegates was precisely analo-
gous to that of the earlier architects who had
designed the structure of the British merchant-
State, with its system of economics, politics and
judicial control; they had to contrive something
that could pass muster as showing a good sem-
blance of popular sovereignty, without the
reality. Madison defined their task explicitly
in saying that the convention's purpose was "to
secure the public good and private rights
against the danger of such a faction [i.e., a democratic faction], and at the same time preserve
the spirit and form of popular government."

Under the circumstances, this was a tremen-
dously large order; and the constitution
emerged, as it was bound to do, as a compro-
mise-document, or as Mr. Beard puts it very
precisely, "a mosaic of second choices," which
really satisfied neither of the two opposing sets
of interests. It was not strong and definite
enough in either direction to please anybody.
In particular, the interests composing the first
division, led by Alexander Hamilton, saw that
it was not sufficient of itself to fix them in anything like a permanent impregnable position

to exploit continuously the groups composing the second division. To do this—to establish the degree of centralization requisite to their purposes—certain lines of administrative management must be laid down, which, once established, would be permanent. The further task therefore, in Madison's phrase, was to "administration" the constitution into such absolutist modes as would secure economic supremacy, by a free use of the political means, to the groups which made up the first division.

This was accordingly done. For the first ten years of its existence the constitution remained in the hands of its makers for administration in directions most favourable to their interests. For an accurate understanding of the newly-erected system's economic tendencies, too much stress can not be laid on the fact that for these ten critical years "the machinery of economic and political power was mainly directed by the men who had conceived and established it." [14] Washington, who had been chairman of the convention, was elected President. Nearly half the Senate was made up of men who had been delegates, and the House of Representatives was

[14] Beard, *op. cit.*, p. 337.

largely made up of men who had to do with the drafting or ratifying of the constitution. Hamilton, Randolph and Knox, who were active in promoting the document, filled three of the four positions in the Cabinet; and all the federal judgeships, without a single exception, were filled by men who had a hand in the business of drafting or of ratification, or both.

Of all the legislative measures enacted to implement the new constitution, the one best calculated to ensure a rapid and steady progress in the centralization of political power was the Judiciary Act of 1789.[15] This measure created a federal supreme court of six members (subsequently enlarged to nine), and a federal district court in each state, with its own complete personnel, and a complete apparatus for enforcing its decrees. The Act established federal over-

[15] The principal measures bearing directly on the distribution of the political means were those drafted by Hamilton for funding and assumption, for a protective tariff, and for a national bank. These gave practically exclusive use of the political means to the classes grouped in the first grand division, the only modes left available to others being patents and copyrights. Mr. Beard discusses these measures with his invariable lucidity and thoroughness, *op. cit.,* ch. VIII. Some observations on them which are perhaps worth reading are contained in my *Jefferson,* ch. V.

sight of state legislation by the familiar device of "interpretation," whereby the Supreme Court might nullify state legislative or judicial action which for any reason it saw fit to regard as unconstitutional. One feature of the Act which for our purposes is most noteworthy is that it made the tenure of all these federal judgeships appointive, not elective, and for life; thus marking almost the farthest conceivable departure from the doctrine of popular sovereignty.

The first chief justice was John Jay, "the learned and gentle Jay," as Beveridge calls him in his excellent biography of Marshall. A man of superb integrity, he was far above doing anything whatever in behalf of the accepted principle that *est boni judicis ampliare jurisdictionem*. Ellsworth, who followed him, also did nothing. The succession, however, after Jay had declined a reappointment, then fell to John Marshall, who, in addition to the control established by the Judiciary Act over the state legislative and judicial authority, arbitrarily extended judicial control over both the legislative and executive branches of the federal

authority; [16] thus effecting as complete and
convenient a centralization of power as the
various interests concerned in framing the con-

[16] The authority of the Supreme Court was disre-
garded by Jackson, and overruled by Lincoln, thus
converting the mode of the State temporarily from an
oligarchy into an autocracy. It is interesting to observe that just such a contingency was foreseen by
the framers of the constitution, in particular by
Hamilton. They were apparently well aware of the
ease with which, in any period of crisis, a quasi-
republican mode of the State slips off into executive
tyranny. Oddly enough, Mr. Jefferson at one time
considered nullifying the Alien and Sedition Acts by
executive action, but did not do so. Lincoln overruled the opinion of Chief Justice Taney that suspen-
sion of the *hubeas corpus* was unconstitutional, and
in consequence the mode of the State was, until 1865,
a monocratic military despotism. In fact, from the
date of his proclamation of blockade, Lincoln ruled
unconstitutionally throughout his term. The doctrine of "reserved powers" was knaved up *ex post
facto* as a justification of his acts, but as far as the
intent of the constitution is concerned, it was obviously a pure invention. In fact, a very good case
could be made out for the assertion that Lincoln's
acts resulted in a permanent radical change in the
entire system of constitutional "interpretation"—that
since his time "interpretations" have not been interpretations of the constitution, but merely of public
policy; or, as our most acute and profound social
critic put it, "th' Supreme Court follows th' iliction
rayturns." A strict constitutionalist might indeed say
that the constitution died in 1861, and one would
have to scratch one's head pretty diligently to refute
him.

stitution could reasonably have contemplated.[17]

We may now see from this necessarily brief survey, which anyone may amplify and particularize at his pleasure, what the circumstances were which rooted a certain definite idea of the State still deeper in the general consciousness. That idea was precisely the same in the constitutional period as that which we have seen prevailing in the two periods already examined—the colonial period, and the eight-year period following the revolution. No-

[17] Marshall was appointed by John Adams at the end of his Presidential term, when the interests grouped in the first division were becoming very anxious about the opposition developing against them among the exploited interests. A letter written by Oliver Wolcott to Fisher Ames gives a good idea of where the doctrine of popular sovereignty stood; his reference to military measures is particularly striking. He says, "The steady men in Congress will attempt to extend the judicial department, and I hope that their measures will be very decided. It is impossible in this country to render an army an engine of government; and there is no way to combat the state opposition but by an efficient and extended organization of judges, magistrates, and other civil officers." Marshall's appointment followed, and also the creation of twenty-three new federal judgeships. Marshall's cardinal decisions were made in the cases of Marbury, of Fletcher, of McCulloch, of Dartmouth College, and of Cohens. It is perhaps not generally understood that as the result of Marshall's efforts, the Supreme

where in the history of the constitutional period do we find the faintest suggestion of the Declaration's doctrine of natural rights; and we find its doctrine of popular sovereignty not only continuing in abeyance, but constitutionally estopped from ever reappearing. Nowhere do we find a trace of the Declaration's theory of government; on the contrary, we find it expressly repudiated. The new political mechanism was a faithful replica of the old disestablished British model, but so far improved

Court became not only the highest law-interpreting body, but the highest law-making body as well; the precedents established by its decisions have the force of constitutional law. Since 1800, therefore, the actual mode of the State in America is normally that of a small and irresponsible oligarchy! Mr. Jefferson, regarding Marshall quite justly as "a crafty chief judge who sophisticates the law to his mind by the turn of his own reasoning," made in 1821 the very remarkable prophecy that "our government is now taking so steady a course as to show by what road it will pass to destruction, to wit: by consolidation first, and then corruption, its necessary consequence. The engine of consolidation will be the federal judiciary; the other two branches the corrupting and corrupted instruments." Another prophetic comment on the effect of centralization was his remark that "when we must wait for Washington to tell us when to sow and when to reap, we shall soon want bread." A survey of our present political circumstances makes comment on these prophecies superfluous.

and strengthened as to be incomparably more
close-working and efficient, and hence presenting incomparably more attractive possibilities
of capture and control. By consequence, therefore, we find more firmly implanted than ever
the same general idea of the State that we have
observed as prevailing hitherto—the idea of an
organization of the political means, an irresponsible and all-powerful agency standing always ready to be put into use for the service of
one set of economic interests as against another.

IV

Out of this idea proceeded what we know as
the "party system" of political management,
which has been in effect ever since. Our purposes do not require that we examine its history in close detail for evidence that it has
been from the beginning a purely bipartisan
system, since this is now a matter of fairly
common acceptance. In his second term Mr.
Jefferson discovered the tendency towards bipartisanship,[18] and was both dismayed and puz-

[18] He had observed it in the British State some
years before, and spoke of it with vivacity. "The

zled by it. I have elsewhere [19] remarked his curious inability to understand how the cohesive power of public plunder works straight towards political bipartisanship. In 1823, finding some who called themselves Republicans favouring the Federalist policy of centralization, he spoke of them in a rather bewildered way as "pseudo-Republicans, but real Federalists." But most naturally any Republican who saw a chance of profiting by the political means

nest of office being too small for all of them to cuddle into at once, the contest is eternal which shall crowd the other out. For this purpose they are divided into two parties, the Ins and the Outs." Why he could not see that the same thing was bound to take place in the American State as an effect of causes identical with those which brought it about in the British State, is a puzzle to students. Apparently, however, he did not see it, notwithstanding the sound instinct that made him suspect parties, and always kept him free from party alliances. As he wrote Hopkinson in 1789, "I never submitted the whole system of my opinions to the creed of any party of men whatever, in religion, in philosophy, in politics, or in anything else where I was capable of thinking for myself. Such an addiction is the last degradation of a free and moral agent. If I could not go to heaven but with a party, I would not go there at all."

[19] *Jefferson*, p. 274. The agrarian-artisan-debtor economic group that elected Mr. Jefferson took title as the Republican party (subsequently re-named Democratic) and the opposing group called itself by the old pre-constitutional title of Federalist.

would retain the name, and at the same time resist any tendency within the party to impair the general system which held out such a prospect.[20] In this way bipartisanship arises. Party designations become purely nominal, and the stated issues between parties become progressively trivial; and both are more and more openly kept up with no other object than to cover from scrutiny the essential identity of purpose in both parties.

Thus the party system at once became in effect an elaborate system of fetiches, which, in order to be made as impressive as possible, were chiefly moulded up around the constitution, and were put on show as "constitutional principles." The history of the whole post-constitutional period, from 1789 to the present day, is an instructive and cynical exhibit of the fate of these fetiches when they encounter the one only actual principle of party action—the

[20] An example, noteworthy only because uncommonly conspicuous, is seen in the behaviour of the Democratic senators in the matter of the tariff on sugar, in Cleveland's second administration. Ever since that incident, one of the Washington newspapers has used the name "Senator Sorghum" in its humorous paragraphs, to designate the typical venal jobholder.

principle of keeping open the channels of access to the political means. When the fetich of "strict construction," for example, has collided with this principle, it has invariably gone by the board, the party that maintained it simply changing sides. The anti-Federalist party took office in 1800 as the party of strict construction; yet, once in office, it played ducks and drakes with the constitution, in behalf of the special economic interests that it represented.[21] The Federalists were nominally for loose construction, yet they fought bitterly every one of the opposing party's loose-constructionist measures —the embargo, the protective tariff and the national bank. They were constitutional nationalists of the deepest dye, as we have seen;

[21] Mr. Jefferson was the first to acknowledge that his purchase of the Louisiana territory was unconstitutional; but it added millions of acres to the sum of agrarian resource, and added an immense amount of prospective voting-strength to agrarian control of the political means, as against control by the financial and commercial interests represented by the Federalist party. Mr. Jefferson justified himself solely on the ground of public policy, an interesting anticipation of Lincoln's self-justification in 1861, for confronting Congress and the country with a like *fait accompli*— this time, however, executed in behalf of financial and commercial interests as against the agrarian interest.

yet in their centre and stronghold, New England, they held the threat of secession over the country throughout the period of what they harshly called "Mr. Madison's war," the War of 1812, which was in fact a purely imperialistic adventure after annexation of Floridan and Canadian territory, in behalf of stiffening agrarian control of the political means; but when the planting interests of the South made the same threat in 1861, they became fervid nationalists again.

Such exhibitions of pure fetichism, always cynical in their transparent candour, make up the history of the party system. Their *reductio ad absurdum* is now seen as perhaps complete—one can not see how it could go further—in the attitude of the Democratic party towards its historical principles of state sovereignty and strict construction. A fair match for this, however, is found in a speech made the other day to a group of exporting and importing interests by the mayor of New York—always known as a Republican in politics—advocating the hoary Democratic doctrine of a low tariff!

Throughout our post-constitutional period

there is not on record, as far as I know, a single instance of party adherence to a fixed principle, *qua* principle, or to a political theory, *qua* theory. Indeed, the very cartoons on the subject show how widely it has come to be accepted that party-platforms, with their cant of "issues," are so much sheer quackery, and that campaign-promises are merely another name for thimblerigging. The workaday practice of politics has been invariably opportunist, or in other words, invariably conformable to the primary function of the State; and it is largely for this reason that the State's service exerts its most powerful attraction upon an extremely low and sharp-set type of individual.[22]

The maintenance of this system of fetiches, however, gives great enhancement to the prevailing general view of the State. In that view, the State is made to appear as somehow

[22] Henry George made some very keen comment upon the almost incredible degradation that he saw taking place progressively in the personnel of the State's service. It is perhaps most conspicuous in the Presidency and the Senate, though it goes on *pari passu* elsewhere and throughout. As for the federal House of Representatives and the state legislative bodies, they must be seen to be believed.

deeply and disinterestedly concerned with great
principles of action; and hence, in addition
to its prestige as a pseudo-social institution, it
takes on the prestige of a kind of moral authority, thus disposing of the last vestige of
the doctrine of natural rights by overspread-
ing it heavily with the quicklime of legalism;
whatever is State-sanctioned is right.   This
double prestige is assiduously inflated by many
agencies; by a State-controlled system of education, by a State-dazzled pulpit, by a meretri-
cious press, by a continuous kaleidoscopic dis-
play of State pomp, panoply and circumstance,
and by all the innumerable devices of electioneering.   These last invariably take their
stand on the foundation of some imposing
principle, as witness the agonized cry now
going up here and there in the land, for a
"return to the constitution."   All this is simply "the interested clamours and sophistry,"
which means no more and no less than it
meant when the constitution was not yet five
years old, and Fisher Ames was observing contemptuously that of all the legislative measures and proposals which were on the carpet
at the time, he scarce knew one that had not

raised this same cry, "not excepting a motion for adjournment."

In fact, such popular terms of electioneering appeal are uniformly and notoriously what Jeremy Bentham called impostor-terms, and their use invariably marks one thing and one only; it marks a state of apprehension, either fearful or expectant, as the case may be, concerning access to the political means. As we are seeing at the moment, once let this access come under threat of straitening or stoppage, the menaced interests immediately trot out the spavined, glandered hobby of "state rights" or "a return to the constitution," and put it through its galvanic movements. Let the incidence of exploitation show the first sign of shifting, and we hear at once from one source of "interested clamours and sophistry" that "democracy" is in danger, and that the unparalleled excellences of our civilization have come about solely through a policy of "rugged individualism," carried out under terms of "free competition"; while from another source we hear that the enormities of *laissez-faire* have ground the faces of the poor, and obstructed entrance into the More Abundant Life.[23]

The general upshot of all this is that we see politicians of all schools and stripes behaving with the obscene depravity of degenerate children; like the loose-footed gangs that infest the railway-yards and purlieus of gas-houses, each group tries to circumvent another with respect to the fruit accruing to acts of public mischief.

[23] Of all the impostor-terms in our political glossary, these are perhaps the most flagrantly impudent, and their employment perhaps the most flagitious. We have already seen that nothing remotely resembling democracy has ever existed here; nor yet has anything resembling free competition, for the existence of free competition is obviously incompatible with any exercise of the political means, even the feeblest. For the same reason, no policy of rugged individualism has ever existed; the most that rugged individualism has done to distinguish itself has been by way of running to the State for some form of economic advantage. If the reader has any curiosity about this, let him look up the number of American business enterprises that have made a success unaided by the political means, or the number of fortunes accumulated without such aid. *Laissez-faire* has become a term of pure opprobrium; those who use it either do not know what it means, or else wilfully pervert it. As for the unparalleled excellences of our civilization, it is perhaps enough to say that the statistics of our insurance-companies now show that four-fifths of our people who have reached the age of sixty-five are supported by their relatives or by some other form of charity.

In other words, we see them behaving in a strictly historical manner. Professor Laski's elaborate moral distinction between the State and officialdom is devoid of foundation. The State is not, as he would have it, a social institution administered in an anti-social way. It is an anti-social institution, administered in the only way an anti-social institution can be administered, and by the kind of person who, in the nature of things, is best adapted to such service.

6

SUCH has been the course of our experience from the beginning, and such are the terms in which its stark uniformity has led us to think of the State. This uniformity also goes far to account for the development of a peculiar moral enervation with regard to the State, exactly parallel to that which prevailed with regard to the Church in the Middle Ages.[1]

---

[1] Not long ago Professor Laski commented on the prevalence of this enervation among our young people, especially among our student-population. It has several contributing causes, but it is mainly to be accounted for, I think, by the unvarying uniformity of our experience. The State's pretensions have been so invariably extravagant, the disparity between them and its conduct so invariably manifest, that one could hardly expect anything else. Probably the protest against our imperialism in the Pacific and the Caribbean, after the Spanish War, marked the last major effort of an impotent and moribund decency. Mr. Laski's comparisons with student-bodies in England and Europe lose some of their force when it is remembered that the devices of a fixed term and an irresponsible executive render the American State peculiarly insensitive to protest and inaccessible to effec-

The Church controlled the distribution of certain privileges and immunities, and if one approached it properly, one might get the benefit of them. It stood as something to be run to in any kind of emergency, temporal or spiritual; for the satisfaction of ambition and cupidity, as well as for the more tenuous assurances it held out against various forms of fear, doubt and sorrow. As long as this was so, the anomalies presented by its self-aggrandizement were more or less contentedly acquiesced in; and thus a chronic moral enervation, too negative to be called broadly cynical, was developed towards its interventions and exactions, and towards the vast overbuilding of its material structure.[2]

A like enervation pervades our society with respect to the State, and for like reasons. It affects especially those who take the State's pretensions at face value and regard it as a social institution whose policies of continuous

tive censure. As Mr. Jefferson said, the one resource of impeachment is "not even a scarecrow."

[2] As an example of this overbuilding, at the beginning of the sixteenth century one-fifth of the land of France was owned by the Church; it was held mainly by monastic establishments.

intervention are wholesome and necessary; and
it also affects the great majority who have no
clear idea of the State, but merely accept it
as something that exists, and never think about
it except when some intervention bears unfavourably upon their interests.   There is
little need to dwell upon the amount of aid
thus given to the State's progress in self-
aggrandizement, or to show in detail or by
illustration the courses by which this spirit-
lessness promotes the State's steady policy of
intervention, exaction and overbuilding.[3]

[3] It may be observed, however, that mere use-and-
wont interferes with our seeing how egregiously the
original structure of the American State, with its system of superimposed jurisdictions and reduplicated
functions, was overbuilt.   At the present time, a
citizen lives under half-a-dozen or more separate over-
lapping jurisdictions, federal, state, county, township,
municipal, borough, school-district, ward, federal district.   Nearly all of these have power to tax him directly or indirectly, or both, and as we all know, the
only limit to the exercise of this power is what can
be safely got by it; and thus we arrive at the principle rather naïvely formulated by the late senator
from Utah, and sometimes spoken of ironically as
"Smoot's law of government"—the principle, as he
put it, that the cost of government tends to increase
from year to year, no matter which party is in power.
It would be interesting to know the exact distribution of the burden of jobholders and mendicant political retainers—for it must not be forgotten that

Every intervention by the State enables
another, and this in turn another, and so on
indefinitely; and the State stands ever ready
and eager to make them, often on its own
motion, often again wangling plausibility for
them through the specious suggestion of interested persons. Sometimes the matter at
issue is in its nature simple, socially necessary,
and devoid of any character that would bring
it into the purview of politics.⁴ For conven-

the subsidized "unemployed" are now a permanent
body of patronage—among income-receiving citizens.
Counting indirect taxes and voluntary contributions
as well as direct taxes, it would probably be not far
off the mark to say that every two citizens are carrying a third between them.

⁴ For example, the basic processes of exchange are
necessary, non-political, and as simple as any in the
world. The humblest Yankee rustic who swaps eggs
for bacon in the country store, or a day's labour for
potatoes in a neighbour's field, understands them
thoroughly, and manages them competently. Their
formula is: goods or services in return for goods or
services. There is not, never has been, and never will
be, a single transaction anywhere in the realm of
"business"—no matter what its magnitude or apparent complexity—that is not directly reducible to
this formula. For convenience in facilitating exchange, however, money was introduced; and money
is a complication, and so are the other evidences of
debt, such as cheques, drafts, notes, bills, bonds, stock-
certificates, which were introduced for the same reason. These complications were found to be exploit-

ience, however, complications are erected on
it; then presently someone sees that these
complications are exploitable, and proceeds to
exploit them; then another, and another, until
the rivalries and collisions of interest thus generated issue in a more or less general disorder.
When this takes place, the logical thing, obviously, is to recede, and let the disorder be settled in the slower and more troublesome way,
but the only effective way, through the operation of natural laws. But in such circumstances recession is never for a moment thought
of; the suggestion would be put down as sheer
lunacy. Instead, the interests unfavourably
affected—little aware, perhaps, how much worse
the cure is than the disease, or at any rate little
caring—immediately call on the State to cut in
arbitrarily between cause and effect, and clear
up the disorder out of hand.[5] The State then

able; and the consequent number and range of State
interventions to "regulate" and "supervise" their
exploitation appear to be without end.

[5] It is one of the most extraordinary things in the
world, that the interests which abhor and dread collectivism are the ones which have most eagerly urged
on the State to take each one of the successive single
steps that lead directly to collectivism. Who urged it
on to form the Federal Trade Commission; to expand

intervenes by imposing another set of complications upon the first; these in turn are found exploitable, another demand arises, another set of complications, still more intricate, is erected upon the first two; [6] and the same sequence is gone through again and again until the recurrent disorder becomes acute enough to open the way for a sharking political adventurer to come forward and, always alleging "necessity, the tyrant's plea," to organize a *coup d'État.* [7]

But more often the basic matter at issue represents an original intervention of the State, an original allotment of the political

the Department of Commerce; to form the Interstate Commerce Commission and the Federal Farm Board; to pass the Anti-trust Acts; to build highways, dig out waterways, provide airway services, subsidize shipping? If these steps do not tend straight to collectivism, just which way do they tend? Furthermore, when the interests which encouraged the State to take them are horrified by the apparition of communism and the Red menace, just what are their protestations worth?

[6] The text of the Senate's proposed banking law, published on the first of July, 1935, almost exactly filled four pages of the *Wall Street Journal!* Really now—now really—can any conceivable absurdity surpass that?

[7] As here in 1932, in Italy, Germany and Russia latterly, in France after the collapse of the Directory, in Rome after the death of Pertinax, and so on.

means. Each of these allotments, as we have
seen, is a charter of highwaymanry, a license
to appropriate the labour-products of others
without compensation. Therefore it is in the
nature of things that when such a license is
issued, the State must follow it up with an
indefinite series of interventions to systematize
and "regulate" its use. The State's endless
progressive encroachments that are recorded
in the history of the tariff, their impudent and
disgusting particularity, and the prodigious
amount of apparatus necessary to give them
effect, furnish a conspicuous case in point.
Another is furnished by the history of our
railway-regulation. It is nowadays the fashion,
even among those who ought to know better,
to hold "rugged individualism" and *laissez-
faire* responsible for the riot of stock-watering,
rebates, rate-cutting, fraudulent bankruptcies,
and the like, which prevailed in our railway-
practice after the Civil War, but they had no
more to do with it than they have with the
precession of the equinoxes. The fact is that
our railways, with few exceptions, did not
grow up in response to any actual economic
demand. They were speculative enterprises

enabled by State intervention, by allotment of
the political means in the form of land-grants
and subsidies; and of all the evils alleged
against our railway-practice, there is not one
but what is directly traceable to this primary
intervention.[8]

So it is with shipping. There was no valid
economic demand for adventure in the carrying trade; in fact, every sound economic consideration was dead against it. It was entered
upon through State intervention, instigated by
shipbuilders and their allied interests; and the
mess engendered by their manipulation of the
political means is now the ground of demand

[8] Ignorance has no assignable limits; yet when one
hears our railway-companies cited as specimens of
rugged individualism, one is put to it to say whether
the speaker's sanity should be questioned, or his integrity. Our transcontinental companies, in particular, are hardly to be called railway-companies, since
transportation was purely incidental to their true
business, which was that of land-jobbing and subsidy-
hunting. I remember seeing the statement a few
years ago—I do not vouch for it, but it can not be far
off the fact—that at the time of writing, the current
cash value of the political means allotted to the
Northern Pacific Company would enable it to build
four transcontinental lines, and in addition, to build
a fleet of ships and maintain it in around-the-world
service. If this sort of thing represents rugged individualism, let future lexicographers make the most
of it.

for further and further coercive intervention.
So it is with what, by an unconscionable stretch
of language, goes by the name of farming.[9]
There are very few troubles so far heard of
as normally besetting this form of enterprise
but what are directly traceable to the State's
primary intervention in establishing a system
of land-tenure which gives a monopoly-right
over rental-values as well as over use-values;

[9] A farmer, properly speaking, is a freeholder who
directs his operations, first, towards making his family, as far as possible, an independent unit, economically self-contained. What he produces over and
above this requirement he converts into a cash crop.
There is a second type of agriculturist, who is not a
farmer, but a manufacturer, as much so as one who
makes woolen or cotton textiles or leather shoes. He
raises one crop only—milk, corn, wheat, cotton, or
whatever it may be—which is wholly a cash crop; and
if the market for his particular commodity goes down
below cost of production, he is in the same bad luck
as the motor-car maker or shoemaker or pantsmaker
who turns out more of his special kind of goods than
the market will bear. His family is not independent;
he buys everything his household uses; his children
can not live on cotton or milk or corn, any more
than the shoe-manufacturer's children can live on
shoes. There is still to be distinguished a third type,
who carries on agriculture as a sort of taxpaying subsidiary to speculation in agricultural land-values. It
is the last two classes who chiefly clamour for intervention, and they are often, indeed, in a bad way;
but it is not farming that puts them there.

and as long as that system is in force, one coercive intervention after another is bound to take place in support of it.[10]

II

Thus we see how ignorance and delusion concerning the nature of the State combine with extreme moral debility and myopic self-interest—what Ernest Renan so well calls *la bassesse de l'homme intéressé*—to enable the steadily accelerated conversion of social power into State power that has gone on from the

[10] The very limit of particularity in this course of coercive intervention seems to have been reached, according to press-reports, in the state of Wisconsin. On 31 May, the report is, Governor La Follette signed a bill requiring all public eating-places to serve two-thirds of an ounce of Wisconsin-made cheese and two-thirds of an ounce of Wisconsin-made butter with every meal costing more than twenty-four cents. To match this for particularity one would pretty well have to go back to some of the British Trade Acts of the eighteenth century, and it would be hard to find an exact match, even there. If this passes muster under the "due process of law" clause—whether the eating-house pays for these supplies or passes their cost along to the consumer—one can see nothing to prevent the legislature of New York, say, from requiring each citizen to buy annually two hats made by Knox, and two suits made by Finchley.

beginning of our political independence. It is a curious anomaly. State power has an unbroken record of inability to do anything efficiently, economically, disinterestedly or honestly; yet when the slightest dissatisfaction arises over any exercise of social power, the aid of the agent least qualified to give aid is immediately called for. Does social power mismanage banking-practice in this-or-that special instance—then let the State, which never has shown itself able to keep its own finances from sinking promptly into the slough of misfeasance, wastefulness and corruption, intervene to "supervise" or "regulate" the whole body of banking-practice, or even take it over entire. Does social power, in this-or-that case, bungle the business of railway-management— then let the State, which has bungled every business it has ever undertaken, intervene and put its hand to the business of "regulating" railway-operation. Does social power now and then send out an unseaworthy ship to disaster —then let the State, which inspected and passed the *Morro Castle,* be given a freer swing at controlling the routine of the shipping trade. Does social power here and there exercise a grinding monopoly over the generation and distribution of electric current—then let the State, which allots and maintains monopoly, come in and intervene with a general scheme of price-fixing which works more unforeseen hardships than it heals, or else let it go into direct competition; or, as the collectivists urge, let it take over the monopoly bodily. "Ever since society has existed," says Herbert Spencer, "disappointment has been preaching, 'Put not your trust in legislation'; and yet the trust in legislation seems hardly diminished."

But it may be asked where we are to go for relief from the misuses of social power, if not to the State. What other recourse have we? Admitting that under our existing mode of political organization we have none, it must still be pointed out that this question rests on the old inveterate misapprehension of the State's nature, presuming that the State is a social institution, whereas it is an anti-social institution; that is to say, the question rests on an absurdity.[11] It is certainly true that the

[11] Admitting that the lamb in the fable had no other recourse than the wolf, one may none the less see that its appeal to the wolf was a waste of breath.

business of *government*, in maintaining "freedom and security," and "to secure these rights," is to make a recourse to justice costless, easy and informal; but *the State*, on the contrary, is primarily concerned with injustice, and its function is to maintain a régime of injustice; hence, as we see daily, its disposition is to put justice as far as possible out of reach, and to make the effort after justice as costly and difficult as it can. One may put it in a word that while government is by its nature concerned with the administration of justice, the State is by its nature concerned with the administration of law—law, which the State itself manufactures for the service of its own primary ends. Therefore an appeal to the State, based on the ground of justice, is futile in any circumstances,[12] for whatever action the State

[12] This is now so well understood that no one goes to a court for justice; he goes for gain or revenge. It is interesting to observe that some philosophers of law now say that law has no relation to justice, and is not meant to have any such relation. In their view, law represents only a progressive registration of the ways in which experience leads us to believe that society can best get along. One might hesitate a long time about accepting their notion of what law is, but one must appreciate their candid affirmation of what it is not.

might take in response to it would be conditioned by the State's own paramount interest,
and would hence be bound to result, as we see
such action invariably resulting, in as great
injustice as that which it pretends to correct,
or as a rule, greater.   The question thus pre-
sumes, in short, that the State may on occasion
be persuaded to act out of character; and this
is levity.

But passing on from this special view of the
question, and regarding it in a more general
way, we see that what it actually amounts to is
a plea for arbitrary interference with the order
of nature, an arbitrary cutting-in to avert the
penalty which nature lays on any and every
form of error, whether wilful or ignorant, voluntary or involuntary; and no attempt at this
has ever yet failed to cost more than it came
to.   Any contravention of natural law, any
tampering with the natural order of things,
must have its consequences, and the only recourse for escaping them is such as entails worse
consequences.   Nature recks nothing of intentions, good or bad; the one thing she will not
tolerate is disorder, and she is very particular
about getting her full pay for any attempt to

create disorder. She gets it sometimes by very indirect methods, often by very roundabout and unforeseen ways, but she always gets it. "Things and actions are what they are, and the consequences of them will be what they will be; why, then, should we desire to be deceived?" It would seem that our civilization is greatly given to this infantile addiction—**greatly** given to persuading itself that it can find some means which nature will tolerate, whereby we may eat our cake and have it; and it strongly resents the stubborn fact that there is no such means.[13]

It will be clear to anyone who takes the trouble to think the matter through, that

[13] This resentment is very remarkable. In spite of our failure with one conspicuously ambitious experiment in State intervention, I dare say there would still be great resentment against Professor Sumner's ill-famed remark that when people talked tearfully about "the poor drunkard lying in the gutter," it seemed never to occur to them that the gutter might be quite the right place for him to lie; or against the bishop of Peterborough's declaration that he would rather see England free than sober. Yet both these remarks merely recognize the great truth which experience forces on our notice every day, that attempts to interfere with the natural order of things are bound, in one way or another, to turn out for the worse.

under a régime of natural order, that is to say
under *government,* which makes no positive
interventions whatever on the individual, but
only negative interventions in behalf of simple
justice—not law, but justice—misuses of social
power would be effectively corrected; whereas
we know by interminable experience that the
State's positive interventions do not correct
them.   Under a régime of actual individualism, actually free competition, actual *laissez-
faire*—a régime which, as we have seen, can
not possibly coexist with the State—a serious
or continuous misuse of social power would
be virtually impracticable.[14]

[14] The horrors of England's industrial life in the last
century furnish a standing brief for addicts of positive intervention.   Child-labour and woman-labour
in the mills and mines; Coketown and Mr. Bound-
erby; starvation wages; killing hours; vile and haz-
ardous conditions of labour; coffin ships officered by
ruffians—all these are glibly charged off by reformers
and· publicists to a régime of rugged individualism,
unrestrained competition, and *laissez-faire.* This is
an absurdity on its face, for no such régime ever
existed in England.   They were due to the State's
primary intervention whereby the population of England was expropriated from the land; due to the
State's removal of the land from competition with
industry for labour.   Nor did the factory system and
the "industrial revolution" have the least thing to do
with creating those hordes of miserable beings.   When

I shall not take up space with amplifying these statements because, in the first place, this has already been thoroughly done by Spencer, in his essays entitled *The Man versus the State;* and, in the second place, because I wish above all things to avoid the appearance of suggesting that a régime such as these statements contemplate is practicable, or that I am ever so covertly encouraging anyone to dwell on the thought of such a régime. Perhaps, some æons hence, if the planet remains so long habitable, the benefits accruing to conquest and confiscation may be adjudged over-costly; the State may in consequence be superseded by government, the political means suppressed, and the fetiches which give nationalism and patriotism their present execrable character

the factory system came in, those hordes were already there, expropriated, and they went into the mills for whatever Mr. Gradgrind and Mr. Plugson of Undershot would give them, because they had no choice but to beg, steal or starve. Their misery and degradation did not lie at the door of individualism; they lay nowhere but at the door of the State. Adam Smith's economics are not the economics of individualism; they are the economics of landowners and mill-owners. Our zealots of positive intervention would do well to read the history of the Enclosures Acts and the work of the Hammonds, and see what they can make of them.

may be broken down. But the remoteness and uncertainty of this prospect makes any thought of it fatuous, and any concern with it futile. Some rough measure of its remoteness may perhaps be gained by estimating the growing strength of the forces at work against it. Ignorance and error, which the State's prestige steadily deepens, are against it; *la bassesse de l'homme intéressé*, steadily pushing its purposes to greater lengths of turpitude, is against it; moral enervation, steadily proceeding to the point of complete insensitiveness, is against it. What combination of influences more powerful than this can one imagine, and what can one imagine possible to be done in the face of such a combination?

To the sum of these, which may be called spiritual influences, may be added the overweening physical strength of the State, which is ready to be called into action at once against any affront to the State's prestige. Few realize how enormously and how rapidly in recent years the State has everywhere built up its apparatus of armies and police forces. The State has thoroughly learned the lesson laid down by Septimius Severus, on his death-bed.

"Stick together," he said to his successors, "pay the soldiers, and don't worry about anything else." It is now known to every intelligent person that there can be no such thing as a revolution as long as this advice is followed; in fact, there has been no revolution in the modern world since 1848—every so-called revolution has been merely a *coup d'État*.[15] All talk of the possibility of a revolution in America is in part perhaps ignorant, but mostly dishonest; it is merely "the interested clamours and sophistry" of persons who have some sort of ax to grind. Even Lenin acknowledged that a revolution is impossible anywhere until the military and police forces become disaffected; and the last place to look for that, probably, is here. We have all seen demonstrations of a disarmed populace, and local riots carried on with primitive weapons, and we have also seen how they ended, as in

[15] When Sir Robert Peel proposed to organize the police force of London, Englishmen said openly that half a dozen throats cut in Whitechapel every year would be a cheap price to pay for keeping such an instrument of potential tyranny out of the State's hands. We are all beginning to realize now that there is a great deal to be said for that view of the matter.

Homestead, Chicago, and the mining districts of West Virginia, for instance. Coxey's Army marched on Washington—and it kept off the grass.

Taking the sum of the State's physical strength, with the force of powerful spiritual influences behind it, one asks again, what can be done against the State's progress in self-aggrandizement? Simply nothing. So far from encouraging any hopeful contemplation of the unattainable, the student of civilized man will offer no conclusion but that nothing can be done. He can regard the course of our civilization only as he would regard the course of a man in a row-boat on the lower reaches of the Niagara—as an instance of Nature's unconquerable intolerance of disorder, and in the end, an example of the penalty which she puts upon any attempt at interference with order. Our civilization may at the outset have taken its chances with the current of Statism either ignorantly or deliberately; it makes no difference. Nature cares nothing whatever about motive or intention; she cares only for order, and looks to see only that her repugnance to disorder shall be vindicated, and that her concern with the regular orderly sequences of things and actions shall be upheld in the outcome. Emerson, in one of his great moments of inspiration, personified cause and effect as "the chancellors of God"; and invariable experience testifies that the attempt to nullify or divert or in any wise break in upon their sequences must have its own reward.

"Such," says Professor Ortega y Gasset, "was the lamentable fate of ancient civilization." A dozen empires have already finished the course that ours began three centuries ago. The lion and the lizard keep the vestiges that attest their passage upon earth, vestiges of cities which in their day were as proud and powerful as ours—Tadmor, Persepolis, Luxor, Baalbek—some of them indeed forgotten for thousands of years and brought to memory again only by the excavator, like those of the Mayas, and those buried in the sands of the Gobi. The sites which now bear Narbonne and Marseilles have borne the habitat of four successive civilizations, each of them, as St. James says, even as a vapour which appeareth for a little time and then vanisheth away. The course of all these civilizations was the

same.   Conquest, confiscation, the erection of
the State; then the sequences which we have
traced in the course of our own civilization;
then the shock of some irruption which the
social structure was too far weakened to resist, and from which it was left too disorgan-
ized to recover; and then the end.

Our pride resents the thought that the great
highways of New England will one day lie
deep under layers of encroaching vegetation,
as the more substantial Roman roads of Old
England have lain for generations; and that
only a group of heavily overgrown hillocks
will be left to attract the archæologist's eye to
the hidden débris of our collapsed skyscrapers.
Yet it is to just this, we know, that our civilization will come; and we know it because we
know that there never has been, never is, and
never will be, any disorder in nature—because
we know that things and actions are what they
are, and the consequences of them will be
what they will be.

But there is no need to dwell lugubriously
upon the probable circumstances of a future
so far distant.   What we and our more nearly
immediate descendants shall see is a steady

progress in collectivism running off into a
military despotism of a severe type. Closer
centralization; a steadily growing bureaucracy;
State power and faith in State power increas-
ing, social power and faith in social power
diminishing; the State absorbing a continually
larger proportion of the national income; production languishing, the State in consequence
taking over one "essential industry" after another, managing them with ever-increasing
corruption, inefficiency and prodigality, and
finally resorting to a system of forced labour.
Then at some point in this progress, a collision of State interests, at least as general and
as violent as that which occurred in 1914, will
result in an industrial and financial disloca-
tion too severe for the asthenic social structure to bear; and from this the State will be
left to "the rusty death of machinery," and
the casual anonymous forces of dissolution will
be supreme.

III

But it may quite properly be asked, if we
in common with the rest of the Western world
are so far gone in Statism as to make this out-

come inevitable, what is the use of a book which merely shows that it is inevitable? By its own hypothesis the book is useless. Upon the very evidence it offers, no one's political opinions are likely to be changed by it, no one's practical attitude towards the State will be modified by it; and if they were, according to the book's own premises, what good could it do?

Assuredly I do not expect this book to change anyone's political opinions, for it is not meant to do that. One or two, perhaps, here and there, may be moved to look a little into the subject-matter on their own account, and thus perhaps their opinions would undergo some slight loosening—or some constriction—but this is the very most that would happen. In general, too, I would be the first to acknowledge that no results of the kind which we agree to call practical could accrue to the credit of a book of this order, were it a hundred times as cogent as this one—no results, that is, that would in the least retard the State's progress in self-aggrandizement and thus modify the consequences of the State's course. There are two reasons, however, one general and one special, why the publication of such a book is admissible.

The general reason is that when in any department of thought a person has, or thinks he has, a view of the plain intelligible order of things, it is proper that he should record that view publicly, with no thought whatever of the practical consequences, or lack of consequences, likely to ensue upon his so doing. He might indeed be thought bound to do this as a matter of abstract duty; not to crusade or propagandize for his view or seek to impose it upon anyone—far from that!—not to concern himself at all with either its acceptance or its disallowance; but merely to record it. This, I say, might be thought his duty to the natural truth of things, but it is at all events his right; it is admissible.

The special reason has to do with the fact that in every civilization, however generally prosaic, however addicted to the short-time point of view on human affairs, there are always certain alien spirits who, while outwardly conforming to the requirements of the civilization around them, still keep a disinterested regard for the plain intelligible law of things, irrespective of any practical end. They have an intellectual curiosity, sometimes touched with emotion, concerning the august order of nature; they are impressed by the contemplation of it, and like to know as much about it as they can, even in circumstances where its operation is ever so manifestly unfavourable to their best hopes and wishes. For these, a work like this, however in the current sense impractical, is not quite useless; and those of them it reaches will be aware that for such as themselves, and such only, it was written.

THE END

17632263R00122

Made in the USA
Lexington, KY
19 September 2012